WHERE TO
IN
AMERICA

KEN WESTCOTT JONES

SETTLE PRESS
HIPPOCRENE BOOKS INC.

© 1991 Ken Westcott Jones
All rights reserved. No part of this publication
may be reproduced or transmitted in any form or
by any means without permission.
First published by Settle Press
10 Boyne Terrace Mews
London W11 3LR

Maps and Plans supplied by Mary Butler, UST TA and AMTRAK

ISBN (Hardback) 0 907070 73 6
     (Paperback) 0 907070 74 4

Published in USA by Hippocrene Books Inc
171 Madison Avenue,
New York N.Y. 10016

ISBN 0-87052-888-2

Printed by Villiers Publications Ltd
26a Shepherds Hill, London N6 5AH

Contents

Acknowledgements

From the innumerable professional and private people who have helped me during some fifty years of travel throughout the United States I must single out a few whose information and assistance over the years has been more than ordinarily useful.

Doreen Willis Bailey came to Britain in 1961 to help set up the first TWA 'Visit America' office in London. She has been at the United States Travel and Tourism Administration in London ever since. Her knowledge is profound and her help with contacts 'on the other side' outstanding.

Mr Beverly Miller was the first Director of the USTS, later USTTA, in Britain (also responsible for Scandinavia). His work has been largely unsung but behind the scenes he was a source of inspiration and friendly helpfulness.

In South Carolina, 'General' Robert G. Liming, the Director of the Division of Tourism, has worked on three itineraries for me during visits to his State. At conventions in America and abroad he wears the uniform of a Confederate General and works hard to promote his fascinating State.

My old friends, for so long heading the New York Convention and Visitors Bureau, Charles Gillett, President, and John P. MacBean, Vice President, put up with my frequent calls over three decades and greatly aided my New York City experiences. They even arranged for me to march over Brooklyn Bridge with a contingent to honour its centenary in 1983.

Introduction – America The Big Country

It was not until 1961 that the United States of America began to take international tourism seriously, and started the 'Visit America' campaign under the wise guidance of Senator Warren Magnuson. Trans World Airlines set up an office in London's Piccadilly to promote the country, and Greyhound – the huge bus network – followed suit. These were the first offices overseas to suggest that people might like to come to America for a holiday.

Shortly afterwards the United States Travel Service, a division of the US Department of Commerce, brought civil servants into the action and opened several offices in Europe. The funding for USTS has never been significant, and after the name was changed to the United States Travel and Tourism Administration it existed on a shoestring. It has recently received half its improved funding from commercial sources, notably AT&T, the communications giant.

Thin though the campaign was, it worked, for there was a vast pent-up demand for holidays in America. Once currency limits in such countries as Britain, West Germany, and Japan were relaxed, visitors swept across the Atlantic or Pacific in waves – on return tickets. It took another ten years before the Immigration officials recognised this and slowly changed their attitude to visitors, having believed they were all coming in order to get jobs and make money without the ordeal of trying to obtain immigrant visas.

In 1989, foreign visitors exceeded six millions, excluding neighbouring Canada and Mexico. Britain was in first place with about two millions, but Japan and West Germany were close behind. It is worth noting that relatively cheap air travel played a big part, and perhaps more importantly made holidays of two weeks duration perfectly practical. The great age of sea travel could not offer this, and although shipping tried hard towards the end of its era, it was vanquished when jet aircraft took over completely from 1962 onwards. The peak year for shipping was in 1957, when 1,037,000 passengers crossed the Atlantic by sea, and 901,000 by air. Today, that number of sea passengers is exceeded every month by those flying, and only one ocean liner plies the route on a somewhat irregular basis (except in summer). Others position for cruising to offer one or two crossings a year, aimed upmarket.

With scheduled airlines, British Airways leads on the Atlantic with flights from London to 16 American cities. It also flies to USA from Manchester and Glasgow. Pan American (first on the Atlantic with 'Clipper' flying boats in 1938) has services from London to 10 American cities, and TWA goes direct to 6, but through its Kansas City "Hub", has one-stop routes to 80 more. North West Airlines, from London (Gatwick) to Boston and the Twin Cities direct, offers 47 more destinations from its Hub at Twin Cities on a one-stop basis.

An enormous number of inclusive holidays (package tours) are offered by European tour operators, with Florida being the prime choice of Britons. The million or more who buy the Florida holidays tend to regard them as a sunnier and warmer destination than the Mediterranean with the added attraction of Disneyworld.

One object of this book is to provide a background to America for those going there for the first time and essentially to entice them to return again and again. Second time visitors always show initiative and a desire to see more of this 'big country', which is inexpensive compared with many European countries (very cheap contrasted with Japan) and easy to travel around.

I have had the good fortune to visit every State in the Union during the course of at least 150 visits spread over five decades. All of them have attractions for visitors, even those in the middle of the Prairies. I have attempted to outline the interesting places and things to do, and at times given my frank personal views. But because it is such a vast country, no one can have been everywhere nor seen everything worth while. Every State is covered in the text, but inevitably much has had to be left out

or has simply escaped my travels.

Like my previous books this book is also for Americans as, contrary to general belief, the majority of Americans are not great travellers. Barely six percent of the 230 million population have passports to travel beyond Canada and Mexico, the Bahamas and Bermuda. Within the country, the family car is the chosen instrument of holidays (and it should be noted that Americans have shorter holidays than most Europeans, often limited to two weeks a year). More than 85 percent of people ride by car, leaving planes, trains and buses to fight for the remaining 15 percent. There are, of course, frequent flyers, but they are the same people all the time, often on business. They are enough, however, to give America the busiest airlines in the world.

More than half of all Americans in the contiguous United States (it is different in Alaska and Hawaii) have not yet flown, while a quarter have never ridden in a train. The ubiquitous car, emanating from the 'Nation on Wheels' promised so long ago by Henry Ford, takes them on their vacations, rarely more than a thousand miles from home. Foreigners want to go further than that, having crossed the Atlantic or Pacific to get there. They also want to see the land at scenic level, at least one way.

For those with wider travel ambitions, be they Americans or visitors from abroad, this book is dedicated.

1.   Choosing a Holiday/Personal Recommendations

Types of choice

Somewhere in the 'big country' that is America even in the depths of winter the sun will be shining and it will be warm. That is the appeal of South Florida, nosing into the Tropics, where beach holidays all year round have attracted so many Europeans, especially Britons, on 'packaged' vacations.

Americans and Canadians flock to Florida during the winter months and have done since Henry Flagler opened up the extremities of the peninsula soon after the turn of the century. These holidaymakers are known as 'Snowbirds'. But if they are looking for steady warmth when the bulk of the land is freezing they might just as easily opt for the Texas Tropical Coast or San Diego and its array of Southern California beaches. Florida happens to be more accessible, better publicized, with abundant facilities, and it is nearer to Europe and the heavily populated areas of the Eastern States. It also has great 'attractions'.

Florida, or at least the extreme South of the State below Palm Beach and extending down the Keys, has become first choice for millions, and is the destination area for almost half the two million Britons visiting America each year. They all choose Florida not simply because of sun and sea, but also on account of the concentrated attractions around what used to be a small and sleepy town in Central Florida – Orlando; in short, Disney World, coupled with MGM, Universal, Sea World, Cyprus Gardens and others. For their sand and sea, there is the Pinellas Sun Coast on the Gulf of Mexico only 45 miles from Orlando, or Miami Beach on the east coast.

For great scenery, one must turn to the West, to the mountains, rivers and canyons. It is a vast area and one cannot hope to see it all even on several extended visits. Most Americans only get two weeks summer vacation, and if they pile the family into a car and 'tour the West' the most they can hope for is 3000 miles of road cruising. It would need four such vacations, all to different areas, to glimpse most of the West.

Coach tours do cover a good deal more ground, and these are particularly popular with Europeans and those from 'Down Under', often doing a Coast to Coast in three weeks. The Grand Canyon ranks high among the sights to see, and almost level with that marvellous natural wonder is the Golden Gate at San Francisco.

New York City has been a tourist Mecca for a century or more, and it remains so, but often not for a whole vacation. A few days in the huge metropolis tend to be followed by a tour of New England (a prime choice in the month of fall foliage) or a trip to Niagara Falls and down to Washington, probably via Philadelphia and the Maryland countryside.

The Swiss, a relatively wealthy nation of individualists, often spend vacations in the United States, usually choosing the late fall period (which coincides with a slack, wet season in their own country prior to the skiing). A prime Swiss choice is the desert of the South West. Many stay at El Paso, or in Tucson and Phoenix, Arizona. Mountains do not impress them, but bright sunshine and dry air with desert vistas appeal greatly. Naturally they visit the Grand Canyon but also spend time at Arizona's other remarkable sites such as Monument Valley, the Petrified Forest, and the Painted Rocks/Gila Bend Country.

Enormous though the distances are, with Europe 'lost' within its borders (New York to Los Angeles is much further than Lisbon to Moscow while Miami to Seattle is more than twice as far as from Stockholm to Istanbul), the cost of travel need not be a deterrent. We see in Chapter Thirteen how the 'go-as-you-please' ticket system works, with determined bus riders, for example, covering a mile for two cents. Flying to a gateway in the East is only one hundred Pounds Sterling less than a round trip to the extreme

West. It is, incidentally, cheaper to fly on an off-season mid-week round trip from London to New York than London to the Shetland Islands.

Choice, therefore, need not be too dependent upon cost nor upon time, but rather the climate sought, the scenery or city to be enjoyed, the people to meet. Lower holiday prices in some areas may compensate for the extra transport fares.
Taking an AMTRAK nationwide USARAILPAS valid for 45 days and giving it the fullest use would result in $1\frac{1}{4}$ cents a mile travel with the 'hotel content' of a sleeping berth adding another five cents a mile, (with careful overnight up-grading).

Remember that with domestic flying, even on the lowest priced 'go-as-you-please' air ticket, overnighting cannot be expected in flight, while the significant costs of getting to and from out-of-town airports has to be added.

There follows a summary 'Which Resort or Which City' guide, in the form of personal rating tables, followed by examples of climatic conditions to assist readers choose (or avoid) particular destinations for their visits.

Personal Recommendations

Obviously a country the size of the United States, with some 230 million people, has something for everyone somewhere. Here are some of my personal selections:

Aircraft Enthusiasts	Reno; Dayton; Harlingen (Texas); Fayetville (NY); Old Rhinebeck Aerodrome (NY)
American Football Fans	All major cities plus Big Bowls in Miami and New Orleans. All major colleges
Artists	Cape Cod; Monterey Peninsula
Beach Lovers	Cape Cod; Florida West Coast; Malibu
Bird Watchers	Aransas (Texas); Florida W. Coast; Everglades; Padre Island (Texas); Minnesota Lakes
Culture Vultures	New York City; Boston; Chicago (Ravinia); Getty Museum (Cal); Washington DC
Gays	New York City; San Francisco
Gamblers	Atlantic City; Reno; Las Vegas
Golfers	Every State but particularly Pinewood NJ; Augusta, Georgia; S. Carolina islands
Gourmets	New York City; New Orleans; Philadelphia
Hikers & Backpackers	All mountain regions particularly Oregon and Utah; Adirondacks (NY)
Horse Racing Devotees	Kentucky; Hialeah (Florida)
Honeymooners	Any quiet lake resort in summer; New York City; Miami Beach; Niagara Falls
Motor Cycle Enthusiasts	Daytona Beach (Florida); Los Angeles
Motor Campers	The entire nation
Motor Racing Fans	Indianapolis; Daytona Beach
Night Lifers	New York City; Las Vegas; Los Angeles
Railway Enthusiasts	138 preserved and steam railroads; W. Maryland; Colorado (longest rides)
Tennis Lovers	Long Island; Hilton Head Island; Florida
Trend Setters	Already 'set' by largest number on Earth; Maine off-shore islands?
Trail Riders	Wyoming; Montana; Texas Hill Country
Wagon-Train Riders	Kansas
Wild Lifers	Yellowstone National Park; Cascade Mts. Upper Michigan Peninsula; Big Bend (Texas High Sierras)

Film buffs will find the studio tours of Hollywood and Orlando very satisfying. **Theatregoers** have a choice of 32 live theatres in New York City (if they can get seats) plus an immense amount of summer stock plays all over New England. HOT RODDERS (the 4 second dash to 200 mph) is 40 years old as a sport; there are 65 tracks. GAINESVILLE, Florida, and California, are leading places.

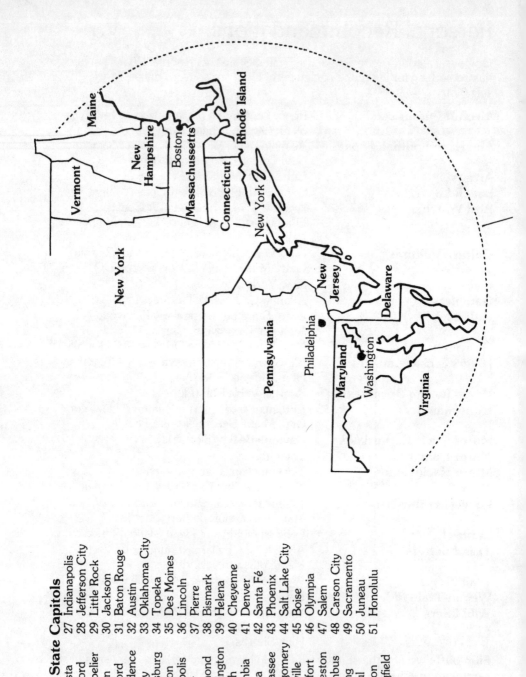

State Capitols

1 Augusta	27 Indianapolis
2 Concord	28 Jefferson City
3 Montpelier	29 Little Rock
4 Boston	30 Jackson
5 Hartford	31 Baton Rouge
6 Providence	32 Austin
7 Albany	33 Oklahoma City
8 Harrisburg	34 Topeka
9 Trenton	35 Des Moines
10 Annapolis	36 Lincoln
11 Dover	37 Pierre
12 Richmond	38 Bismark
13 Washington	39 Helena
14 Raleigh	40 Cheyenne
15 Columbia	41 Denver
16 Atlanta	42 Santa Fé
17 Talahassee	43 Phoenix
18 Montgomery	44 Salt Lake City
19 Nashville	45 Boise
20 Frankfort	46 Olympia
21 Charleston	47 Salem
22 Columbus	48 Carson City
23 Lansing	49 Sacramento
24 St Paul	50 Juneau
25 Madison	51 Honolulu
26 Springfield	

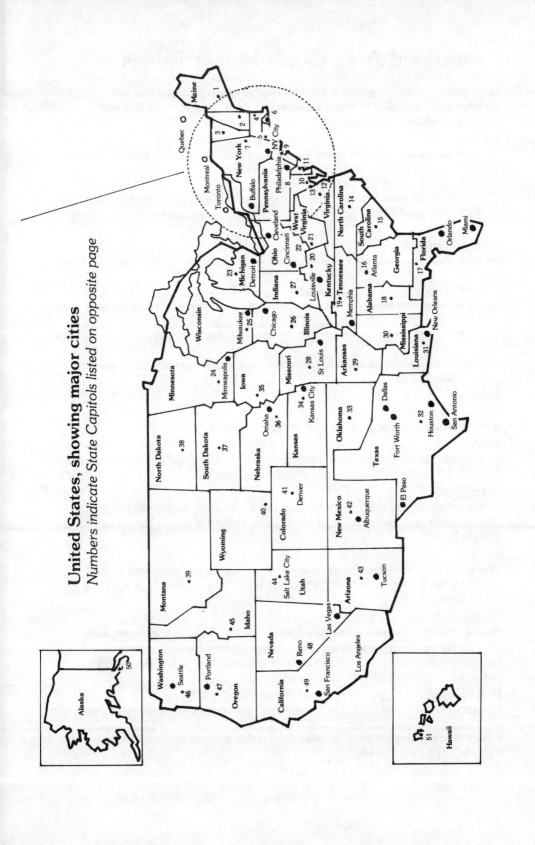

United States, showing major cities
Numbers indicate State Capitols listed on opposite page

Resort and Area Guide Rating Tables

Each has different ingredients, and the overall rating is a personal assessment on how these combine to provide a good mixture for an interesting and satisfying holiday or general visit.

Flights

★★★★★ indicates frequent direct flights from London or other European cities.

★★★★ means reasonably frequent direct flights.

★★★ direct flights but not every day.

★★ at least once a week direct and an easy single change of flight daily

★ No direct flights but one or two changes giving access at least 5 times weekly.

Public Transport

★★★★★ indicates an excellent urban bus, tram or metro system and adequate to good rail and bus access.

★★★★ a good urban transport network plus reasonable bus or train access.

★★★ moderate bus, tram or ferry services, with train and bus access at least daily.

★★ limited public buses in the city, and long distance buses and trains once daily.

★ Poor or non-existent urban buses, and a bus or train three times weekly.

Beaches

These may be sea, lake or river, and are graded according to sand, facilities, warmth in summer, access, and water sport possibilities.

Scenery

Graded according to spectacle, from superb mountains and glaciers (★★★★★) to flat and dull (★).

Attractions

All important for Americans on holiday and increasingly so for visitors from abroad, these are man-made and range from ★★★★★ (such as Disneyworld) to ★ (very limited).

Sites

This includes pre-historic Indian villages, Civil War battlefields, and natural wonders, from ★★★★★ (a great deal of interest in the vicinity) to ★ (nothing much to see).

Eating Out

Americans eat out more than any other peoples in the world, so every town and city has plenty of places to enjoy food. Rated ★★★★★ for wide variety of restaurants and cafes with good food and opportunities to sample regional dishes to ★ very little choice beyond fast foods.

Nightlife

Obviously, New York City, Las Vegas and Reno are the most vigorous late night spots in the world. Areas with near-Prohibition will be rated ★ or nil. Where there is only a couple of discos for teenagers and one expensive nightclub, the rating is ★★.

Climate

Ten of the world's twelve major natural climatic regions are included in USA – for details see Chapter 17.

Rating Tables

City or Area	Flights	Public Transport	Beaches	Scenery	Attractions	Sites	Eating Out	Night Life
New England	★★★★	★★★	★★★	★★★★	★★★	★★★	★★★★	★★
New York City	★★★★★	★★★★★	★★★	★★	★★★★	★	★★★★★	★★★★★
Baltimore	★★★★	★★★★	★★★	★★	★★★	★★	★★★	★★★
Washington DC	★★★★	★★★★★	★	★★	★★★★★	★★	★★★	★★
Niagara Falls	★★	★★	★	★★	★★★★	★★★★★	★★★	★★
Charleston S.Car.	★	★★	★★★★	★	★★★★	★★★	★★★	★★
Florida Gulf Coast	★★★★	★★	★★★★★	★	★★★★★	★	★★★	★★★
Florida Southeast	★★★★★	★★★★	★★★★★	★	★★★★★	★★	★★★★	★★★
Atlanta	★★★★	★★★★	★	★★	★★★	★★	★★★★	★★
New Orleans	★★	★★★★	★★	★★	★★★	★★	★★★★	★★★★★
Houston, Texas	★★★	★★	★★★	★	★★★★	★★	★★★	★★
Dallas/Ft. Worth	★★★★	★★	★	★	★★★★	★	★★★	★★
Chicago	★★★★	★★★★	★★	★	★★★	★	★★★★	★★★★
Twin Cities	★★★	★★	★	★★	★★★	★	★★★	★★
Kansas City	★★	★	★	★	★	★★	★★	★
Denver	★★★	★★	★	★★★★★	★★★	★★	★★	★★
Salt Lake City	★★	★★★	★★	★★★★★	★★★	★★	★★	Nil
Las Vegas	★★	★★	★★★	★★★★	★★★★★	★★	★★★★	★★★★★
Reno	★	★	★★	★★★★	★★★★★	★★	★★★★	★★★★★
San Francisco	★★★★★	★★★★★	★★	★★★★	★★★★	★★	★★★	★★★
Seattle/Portland	★★★★	★★★★★	★★★	★★★★★	★★★	★★★	★★★★	★★
Los Angeles	★★★★★	★★★	★★★★	★★★★	★★★★★	★★★	★★★★	★★★★★
San Diego	★★★	★★★★	★★★★★	★★★	★★★★★	★★	★★★	★★★
NW Wyoming	★	★	★	★★★★★	★★★	★★★	★	★ (*)
Phoenix, Ariz.	★★	★★	★	★★★★	★★	★★★★	★★	★★

* Mainly during ski season.

NEW YORK and NEW ENGLAND

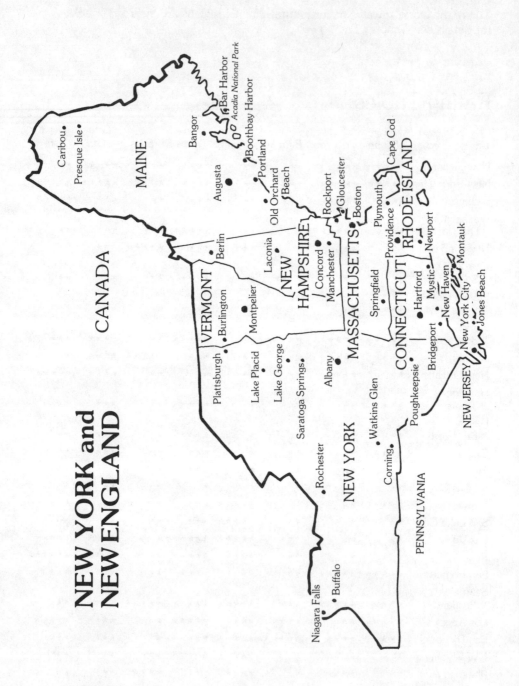

CANADA

MAINE

Caribou•
Presque Isle•

Bangor•

Augusta•

Bar Harbor
Acadia National Park
Boothbay Harbor

Portland•
Old Orchard Beach•

VERMONT

Berlin•

Burlington•
Montpelier•

Laconia•

NEW HAMPSHIRE

Concord•
Manchester•

Rockport•
Gloucester•
Boston•

MASSACHUSETTS

Springfield•

CONNECTICUT

Hartford•

Plattsburgh•

Lake Placid•
Lake George•

Saratoga Springs•
Albany•

Providence•
RHODE ISLAND
Newport•

Plymouth•

Cape Cod

Mystic•
New Haven•
Bridgeport•

Montauk•
New York City•
Jones Beach•

NEW YORK

Watkins Glen•

Poughkeepsie•

NEW JERSEY

Corning•

Rochester•

PENNSYLVANIA

Niagara Falls•
Buffalo•

2. New York and New England

New York State, Massachusetts, Maine, New Hampshire, Vermont, Connecticutt, Rhode Island

New York

Taking a bite of 'The Big Apple' is still the major attraction of a visit to the United States by foreigners, or a trip by Americans going East. Despite the reported crime on the streets, the drug problem with some 18 percent of the population supposedly hooked on narcotics, the dirt and crowds, the brushes with bankruptcy, New York City remains a magnet.

This is an electrifying place with its own inimitable atmosphere, a city with many of the greatest man-made sights in the world. To know it is to enjoy a love-hate relationship; just to glimpse it for a day is a rewarding experience. The first-time visitor, however much he or she may know from movies and TV about New York, must be armed with facts and up to date maps. So the essential priority is a visit to the New York Visitors and Convention Bureau at Columbus Circle, top of Eighth Avenue and Central Park. All kinds of useful literature about the city is there for free, including vital subway and bus maps.

At the very least there are three things a visitor must do however short of time:- take a cruise by Circle Line (boats start at Pier 83 on the West Side) around Manhattan Island passing under all 19 bridges; ascend the Empire State Building or the even taller World Trade Center Downtown; ride the Staten Island Ferry from Battery across the Harbour on the world's cheapest boat trip.

Transport in New York City costs $1.25, regardless of distance. The Subway system, gleaned from map studies and a grasp of the lettered routes (the 'A Train' is real enough), can provide 30 or more miles for the fixed fare. Passengers need a token, bought at a booth before entering the turnstiles. Buses are frequent but get snarled up in traffic and can be slow, stopping every other block for riders and at every other block for traffic lights. Taxis are all yellow, no longer cheap and often unpleasant but safer at night than walking alone. Never walk after dark West of Ninth Avenue, nor in Central Park.

Most visitors want to see a Broadway Show. There are no longer any live theatres on Broadway itself, they are all on side streets but the title remains. Costs get higher and higher, with 45 Dollars the normal for a seat in the house regardless of location, and much more for popular musicals. But you can get half price by lining up at a booth on the day of the show – the present ones are at 47th Street and Broadway and 100 Williams Street. 'Off-Broadway' show tickets are also sold at these booths.

New York State

Albany is the capital of New York State, 142 miles up the Hudson River, and the 2½ hour trip to this city should be made by train. The fairly frequent AMTRAK service runs along the valley of the Hudson, clinging to the banks and showing off the marvellous scenery of this 'Rhine of North America', complete with castles, and not forgetting the tremendous pile of West Point Military Academy on the left bank about 50 miles from New York. Hyde Park, where President Roosevelt is buried, is on the right bank about 30 miles further.

Niagara Falls

New York State, known as the Empire State, is too vast to see completely without spending weeks, but an extension westwards from Albany to Niagara Falls (about five hours by rail or road) results in the ultimate scenic experience. The Falls are greatly commercialised on both the American and Canadian shores. The Horseshoe Falls are best seen on the Canadian side, but a vital necessity is to carry a passport or identity document if going across. Foreigners who may cross the Falls bridges cannot return to the United States without a valid passport (and a visa in it where required).

New England

Although the hinterland is similar and the glorious colours of Fall (autumn) can be almost equally magnificent, New York is not part of New England. That region comprises six States, three of them bordering New York. The six are Massachusetts, Maine, New Hampshire, Vermont, Connecticut and Rhode Island (smallest State in the Union).

Massachusetts/Boston

Boston is the chief city, 232 miles Northeast of New York, and was founded in 1630 by the Massachusetts Bay Company of London (not by the Pilgrim Fathers who landed at New Plymouth, 60 miles South and ten years earlier). There were waves of mainly English immigrants who quickly spread out to found townships with very English names. So rapidly did Boston grow that by 1720 it was five times larger than Dutch-founded but British-captured New York (Nieuw Amsterdam under the Dutch). Today, despite about three million people in its wide metropolitan area (including a big Irish element), Boston is only a third the size of the giant on the Hudson.

Plymouth (Mayflower)

Britons always seem very interested in American history, especially the founding days. Hundreds of thousands of them have visited the replica "Mayflower" at her moorings in Plymouth, and the re-created Plimoth Plantation three miles away, which straggles down a hillside with authentic plants, flowers and animals (bred back) from the 1627 period. Actors at both conduct themselves true to period in garb, accent and knowledge, never mentioning Boston, for that city is, for them, still three years in the future.

If planning a visit to this historic region, there is a large two-storey motel called "Pilgrim Sands", right on the beach, well located for the Plimoth Plantation (this is deliberately mispelt since the first Governor did it that way). There are 66 rooms and the owner, Tom Bradley, is a former schoolmaster–historian who enjoys telling both Britons and Americans about the unfolding of the 17th century in his part of New England. Plymouth also has a large and tasteful Sheraton for those aiming to pay more.

Cape Cod

Land jutting out into the Atlantic in the form of a giant fish hook a bit to the South of Plymouth is Cape Cod, for over a century a favourite summer place for holidaymakers. Digging the Cape Cod Canal some 60 years ago made it an island, but two bridges (one carrying both road and rail) link it to mainland Massachusetts. All along the North Shore of Cape Cod there is careful preservation, some of the restored or well maintained buildings dating back to 1650, while the South shore is more commercialised, where Hyannis is a relative metropolis. Hyannis Port is renowned for its 'Kennedy Compound', and on high ground the John F. Kennedy memorial strikes a sombre note.

Old inns abound on Cape Cod, but the most charming and authentic of all is at West Barnstable on the North Shore, less than a mile from Barnstable Harbour where whales disport themselves in great numbers. The Ashley Manor dates back to 1699 but has more modern extensions. It is run by Donald and Fay Bain who gave up corporate life in New York City to work 12 or more hours a day catering for their small number of discriminating guests (there are just six suites in colonial style). The turn-over is usually daily, and – although it is highly desirable to book in advance – chance callers may be lucky.

At the very tip of Cape Cod is Provincetown, a picturesque community where the Pilgrim Fathers first landed in 1620. They used their shallop survey boat to cross the bay to a better settlers venue at Plymouth,

and "Mayflower" crossed a few days later on seeing their smoke signal. Yes, the hospitable Indians helped – at that stage! The tallest granite structure in America rears up above the quaint roofs of Provincetown as the Pilgrim Memorial.

Maine

While gentle Cape Cod with its 42 beaches of white sand and soft countryside is New England, so is Maine, a rugged northern land of rocky coves and headlands facing a colder Atlantic. There are more than 300 islands off-shore, sometimes fog-shrouded and mysterious. The State contains what was once the most exclusive resort of all, Bar Harbour. This was totally destroyed by fire in 1947 but is now functioning again as a less fashionable place.

Maine is the largest of the New England states, the northern part of it being wilderness, with Mount Kathadin (5268 feet) rearing high above the Baxter National Park. The extreme North of Maine does not quite reach to the 49th parallel where it borders with Canada's New Brunswick and Quebec Provinces, but its eastern extremity at the town of Calais (pronounced 'Kallas' by the locals) is the furthest East point of mainland USA. For this reason, the inhabitants of Maine are called "Down Easters".

Fall starts early up in Maine and winter is severe, while spring comes late. Summer, however, is a delightful time of year. This used to attract almost everyone who could afford the trip from the big sweltering cities like New York and Washington. Somehow, a summer place was bought or rented, from a millionaire's "cottage" (they always called them cottages even when there were 70 rooms and ten servants) to a shack on a rocky end of shore. Air conditioning in universal use ended much of that profitable tourist traffic. There was no longer any need of Maine's cool sea breezes (or New Brunswick's for that matter) to induce sleep. Machines take care of it now, whether it is Florida in summer or an apartment in an airless section of Philadelphia.

The devoted still come to Maine, though, and it is a favourite of people seeking quiet and nature. In mid-Maine in the small, tidy village of Bethel you can find the Bethel Country Club, with wonderful views towards New Hampshire's White Mountains. The Club is open to visitors who enjoy good beds, splendid meals, and golf on the 18 hole course at inclusive rates which are probably the least expensive and best value in the Northeast.

Largest and finest of the shore inns of Maine is Black Point at Prout's Neck, a few miles South of Portland, Maine's commercial city and largest population centre (200,000 in the metropolitan area). Black Point has been in the same family for many years, and is an established favourite, frequently full all of the peak Fall colour season. It is a complete American plan establishment with superb meals, but there are numerous inns along or close to the rugged shores which do bed and breakfast at modest rates. Many of them are restored old homes; few are younger than a century. A snag is that too many are 'chintzy' and ban smoking.

Capital of Maine is Augusta, a pretty city of typically small size as a Government centre, having some 22,000 people (and that includes Hallowell, two miles away, where surely the greatest concentration of antique shops in the East can be

visited). The capitol's dome is impressive with its white Hallowell granite high above deep green surrounding trees. Augusta was founded in 1624, very early, but Cabot and his followers found the Maine coast in 1498.

Down on Maine's southern coast, half way between Kittery, on the New Hampshire border, and Portland, is Kennebunckport, famed in recent years as the summer home of President Bush. The beach of white sand is one of the best in the State but presidential security has interfered with one end of it. However, Kennebunck itself, a few miles inland, has been known to transport buffs for decades as the home of the largest tramway and trolley museum in America, if not the world. Trams from all over, including Liverpool and Hamburg, Vienna and Montreal, are displayed there with American trams from years past. They make a run under the wires of up to two miles.

New Hampshire

Neighbouring New Hampshire, which has a short strip of coastline around the port and naval base of Portsmouth, is a granite land, sparsely inhabited, with dramatic mountains in the Northeast where Mount Washington rises to just under 7000 feet. This summit, the windiest on Earth, is reached by the world's oldest steam cog railway. Amid the forests at the base of this range is the Mount Washington Hotel in the village of Bretton Woods where a financial agreement was made in 1947 which held the world's currencies stable at fixed rates for more than 20 years.

The Upper Connecticut River Valley is the most attractive part of New Hampshire, especially in September with bright warm days and chilly

18

nights which make the incredible Fall colours the best in all New England.

Vermont State is across the river to the West. Dartmouth College was founded in 1700 close to the river, and the small town of Hanover is part of the University campus, perhaps the loveliest of all seats of learning. New England has many pleasant tree-shaded college towns, but none approach Hanover with its red bricks and white roofs, tall trees and great halls of Academe, the whole complex surrounded by splendid sports fields and backed by wooded hills. At the annual Dartmouth Convocation in September the large student body lifts its voice to sing of the granite hills of New Hampshire, the University song.

Vermont

Nearby White River Junction is the limit of useful public transportation in northern New England. Beyond it is a matter of one train a day or a couple of Vermont Transit buses, while across in Maine only two Greyhound buses a day go to Augusta and on to Bangor and Bar Harbour. A rental car is needed for effective touring in this large region, although there are shared taxi arrangements at some coastal and inland resorts in summer and autumn.

Vermont is the archetypal New England State, a land of rich farms and forests, quiet and sparsely populated. This is where one comes across the largest number of surviving covered bridges, those enchanting wooden structures across rivers great and small, built mainly because the roof stops ice thickening on the roadway. The longest covered bridge in New England, indeed in USA spans the Connecticut River between Cornish, New Hampshire and Windsor, Vermont, 460 feet long. There are less than 500 covered bridges remaining,

out of an estimated one-time 3000.

The capital of Vermont, Montpelier, is a delight, a lovely little city with barely 8000 people whose golden domed capitol is set among thick woods which turn rich red and gold in Fall. There is one big city in the State, over on the eastern shore of massive Lake Champlain, called Burlington, where the State University is located. The train is at nearby Essex Junction.

Middlebury is Vermont's closest approach to Hanover, New Hampshire, as a college town, its one main street lined with fine trees, its shops and boutiques in colonial style, selling books, clothes and antiques. The historic Middlebury Inn serves typical New England meals in its beautiful old dining room, or else on a tree-shaded patio in warm weather.

In recent years, skiing has become very big business in snow areas of the United States, and Vermont has been sharing in the boom. Some of America's best skiing is at Stowe and Killington. The name Vermont means, of course, Green Mountain, and it is the range of that name which provides the snowslopes, 56 developed areas. Ethan Allen is the big historical name here, a powerful figure from the War of Independence who led his 'Green Mountain Boys' to capture Fort Ticonderoga from the British, in 1775.

Mountain Ranges
Where the White Mountains are the high point of New Hampshire and the Greens the backbone of Vermont, the Berkshires are the great rolling forested hills of West Massachusetts. Their summits do not exceed 2400 feet but they have an enchantment which endears them to the people of New England (who are the real 'Yankies'). In their midst a few miles South of Pittsfield – under the 2124

foot bulk of Yokun Seat, lies Tanglewood, the famous symphonic festival site of the Berkshires. Summer concerts here are out-of-doors with picnics, touches of Ravinia and Glyndebourne in the Massachusetts hills.

The Red Lion Inn, nestling amid the Berkshires close to Stockbridge, is an unspoiled 1773 hostelry, run for years by John and James Fitzpatrick, people associated with Berkshire summer stock theatre. The food in their restaurant brings customers from many miles away.

Connecticut/Rhode Island

Connecticut and its neighbour, Rhode Island, are together smaller than any of the other four New England states. The West part of Connecticut is upmarket rural commuterland, with frequent electric train services from such places as Westport and Greenwich to New York. The shoreline has several big ports including New London, where there is a whaling museum, while at Mystic there is a recreated 19th century port complete with sailing ships. The East of the State is rural, with big farms, but Hartford, the capital, is a major city, the insurance headquarters of America, housing the head (home) offices of two dozen companies. The magnificent Capitol is a blend of French chateau and a classical Statehouse with gold dome.

Providence, Rhode Island's capital, situated where the Seekonk River enters Narragansett Bay, has two of the five largest domes in the world. One is the white Georgia marble creation on top of the huge Capitol building, the other crowns the Cathedral of St Peter and Paul. Much local industry includes cotton spinning; this is where processes

poached from 18th century Lancashire came to rest and prosper.

The city is able to show the largest collection of early American homes, found on Benefit Street. It is the site of Brown University, one of the 'Ivy League' greats, founded in 1764 (going West, the next 'Ivy League' is Yale, at New Haven, Connecticut, and heading northeast it is Harvard, outside Boston).

The shorelines of Connecticut and Rhode Island have many good beaches facing the waters of Long Island Sound, Black Island Sound, and the open Atlantic. These are yachting waters, Newport on Rhode Island, 35 miles South of Providence, being the yachting capital of America, the start and finish of many great races including the Newport–Bermuda, and a century of America Cup contests. It was at Newport that the social elite at the turn of the century built their summer homes, some of them actually giant mansions – "Breakers" of Vanderbilt fame having 75 rooms and an indoor staff of 30 servants. Restored and maintained, they are all open to the public at a fee.

Coastal islands

No mention of New England can pass without a comment on its islands living in a time warp – Martha's Vineyard and Nantucket. Both are reached by ferry from Woods Hole, Mass., and recall old whaling days, retaining the atmosphere, houses, and shops of the 1800's. Other islands differ in that highlife seekers as well as regular holiday crowds muster on their shores from June to Labor Day. Block Island, Fire Island and Long Island are three of them (the latter part of New York State). There are two ferry routes from Connecticut to Long Island (from New London to Orient Point and from

Bridgeport to Port Jefferson) and two to Block Island (from Point Judith, Rhode Island, and from Newport). To millions, Long Island means Brooklyn and Queens; to the rich it is the Hamptons; to ecologists it is Montauk Point at the eastern end.

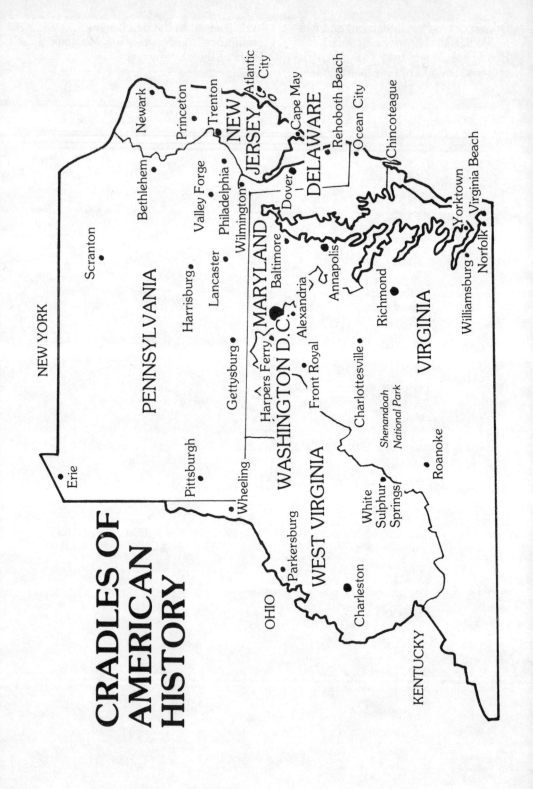

CRADLES OF
AMERICAN
HISTORY

3.   Cradles of American History

Pennsylvania, Delaware, New Jersey, Maryland, West Virginia, Virginia, Washington DC

Philadelphia

Philadelphia, capital of Pennsylvania, has the Liberty Bell and in the minds of most Americans, is the cradle of Independence history. Even more than Boston, Massachusetts, the cities of Philadelphia, Annapolis (Maryland), and Washington DC, reflect the birth of the Republic and its traditions.

Up to 1776, of course, American and British history were intertwined. Even the early settlements were seen as British innovations inspired by monarchs from across the ocean or by merchant venturer companies based in London. But after the Declaration of Independence, things changed. Annapolis, Maryland, became the first effective Capital of the new United States, in 1785, and in 1790 Philadelphia became capital, until facilities in a new city, to be named Washington, were adequate, and these were ready enough for a meeting of Congress in November 1800.

So there were three capitals within 150 miles of each other in this triangle of American history. There was to be a fourth about 115 miles South of Washington, from 1861 to 1865, when Richmond, capital of Virginia, became the Confederate Capital.

Boston, already 146 years old when Independence was declared, was never considered for a capital role in the Federal concept, being too far away in the days of horse-drawn or sailing ship transport. New York City, known as Nieuw Amsterdam under the Dutch until it was ceded to Britain in 1674, was never in the running for Government, although it was already – as a major port – the commercial capital of the eastern seaboard.

Americans treat Philadelphia with a special reverence, for it was here on what is now Independence Mall that the first Bill of Rights and the Constitution were drafted, and the Declaration of Independence signed. Most of the buildings are still there, carefully restored. A new glass pavilion houses the famous Liberty Bell, moved a decade ago from Independence Hall so that more visitors could see it and gather around it. This Bell was cast in England, and taken to Philadelphia (then the major city of all the British colonies) to mark the 50th anniversary of the Commonwealth of Pennsylvania and it reached the city in 1752. Although not an American product it became a symbol of liberty and to prevent it falling into British hands in 1777 it was moved upriver and hidden at Allentown. It has been cracked on at least three occasions by ringing at ceremonies, the last time in 1835.

William Penn and his Quakers founded Pennsylvania in 1681 at the confluence of the Schuylkill and Delaware Rivers, although some Swedish and Dutch settlers had been farming since 1643 and 1655 respectively. Penn created Philadelphia, the 'City of Brotherly Love', and it expanded more quickly than any other among the British colonies (Boston disputes this).

Today the population is just over two millions, by far the largest in the State, although Pittsburgh, the second city, has over 600,000. There are important suburbs spreading along what is still called the 'Philadelphia Main Line', an expression denoting affluent families with 'old' money who live in elegant surroundings near the former Pennsylvania Railroad's four track line to the Allegheny Mountains and beyond. Their offspring go to private schools, attend 'Ivy League' colleges, become doctors, lawyers, stockbrokers and the like. There are more crowded suburbs to the South and North.

Modern Philadelphia has some fine new buildings, but none are outstandingly high-rise due to a law which does not permit any structure to be built higher than William Penn's statue on domed City Hall, which reaches 548 feet. The city and its suburbs are extremely well served by public transport, using the largest tram (trolley) system in the United States, some of the routes passing under the busiest city streets by cut-and-cover subways. Next to Belgium's coastal tram service Philadelphia has the longest routes in the world. There are also deep level subways and suburban trains, the International Airport being served particularly well. Buses run where there are no trams, some of them operating on special pathways along streets freed from other traffic. SEPTA (South East

Pennsylvania Transportation Authority) is the controlling body which does a fine job and even extends its links into neighbouring New Jersey.

Atlantic City

Atlantic City is only 60 miles away, on the coast of New Jersey. A popular seaside resort at the turn of the century noted for its famous three mile long Boardwalk, it became seriously run-down after World War II but has been revived as a 'Las Vegas of the East' with its big hotels transformed into gambling and entertainment complexes. A railway has been upgraded since 1988, with frequent AMTRAK trains running from Philadelphia's 30th Street station over the 67 miles via Lindenwold in New Jersey. Trains take 80 minutes. But visitors might like to know of a 'free' way of going to Atlantic City. This is by motor coach, in several competing lines, starting from various points in Philadelphia in the morning, returning late afternoon. The fare is ten Dollars but on arrival at a Casino each passenger is given ten Dollars' worth of coin, ostensibly for gaming but no law requires the money to be used in this manner.

New Jersey

Called the Garden State, it was the 3rd of the 13 colonies to ratify the Constitution (in 1787). More than 100 battles were fought during the War of Independence, and General Washington crossed the Delaware River from New Jersey on Christmas Day, 1776.

Trenton is the Capitol, an uninspiring city of some 110,000 people, its best feature the Capitol Building with its 145 feet high Golden Dome. The city is facing the Delaware River, and became capital in 1790.

24

New York- Brooklyn Bridge

Albany (N.Y.)
Capitol of New York State

Baltimore (Maryland)
The renowned inner harbour

Philadelphia (Pennsylvania)
Independence Hall -
Liberty Bell Pavilion

Chicago (Illinois) Civic Centre

Amish (Ohio) - A religious sect
relying on horses and buggies

Charleston (S. Carolina)
Downtown ante-bellum houses

S. Carolina
Most southerly covered bridge

Newark has become a major airport served by flights from Britain and Europe, only 10 miles from New York. There is much industry and dereliction in this area, but rural parts of the State are attractive, and there is even a "Pine Barren" wilderness.

Pennsylvania

Pennsylvania is a State worth touring in some detail by car. The Allegheny Mountains make a broad sweep through the land, the enormous forests an amazing sight as deciduous and evergreen trees cover the landscape as far as the eye can see from any overlook upcountry. The Allegheny range presented a severe problem to the settlers heading West and especially to the early railway builders. The mountains were conquered by rail engineers who constructed world-famous Horseshoe Curve about six miles West of the city of Altoona on the way to Pittsburgh. The Curve was designated a National Historic Landmark in 1966 and may be viewed by means of a steps access from the nearby highway. It is a four track main line here which climbs at a two percent grade, the Horseshoe about 1400 feet across but a mile around and climbs about a thousand feet. Opened in 1854 it cleared the way West and is still considered the finest piece of railway engineering in America. Look out for the preserved Pennsylvania Railroad K.4 Pacific which sits at the Summit, an engine retired after running more than two million miles and negotiating the Horseshoe Curve more than 9000 times. But it may be away from site on special historic duties.

Harrisburg is the capital of Pennsylvania, a fine city with a domed capitol building overlooking the lovely Susquehanna River. It is 103 miles from Philadelphia. Nearby, visited by any number of city tours, is Gettysburg, site of the great Civil War battle in 1863 which saw the Confederate forces turned back from their deepest penetration North. It was here after the battle that Abraham Lincoln delivered his short speech ("the World will little note what we say here" but it did and still does), having written it on the back of an envelope during the train journey from Washington.

Coming down from Horseshoe Curve the railway, joining the highway, reaches Johnstown, site of the second worst natural disaster ever to hit the United States (the worst was the Galveston hurricane of 1900). The wall of water which struck the city and destroyed it in less than ten minutes of a late May day in 1889 was caused by incredibly heavy rain bursting an earth dam. There is still danger from floods in this iron and steel city but numerous walls and other precautionary structures should prevent anything like the loss of life (more than 2,200 perished in 1889) in a future inundation.

Pennsylvania has no access to the Atlantic Coast, which is occupied by Delaware, but it does have a shoreline on Lake Erie in the West. This was where the 1825 Erie Canal ended, making a Great Lakes port for Pennsylvania, plus water transport to New York and Philadelphia, with links to Baltimore and Washington by the Chesapeake and Ohio Canal.

Delaware

"First State" is what next-door Delaware often calls itself. This small State, only about 2000 square miles, was first settled by Swedes at what is now Wilmington in 1638. The Dutch came in 1651, wiping out the Swedes, but the British took the whole place in

1664, to hold it for 112 years. Then, in 1776, General George Washington crossed the Delaware . . .

The Delaware River gives its name to the State. It is 390 miles long, rising amid the high points of New York State's Catskills, but it is always marking a border all the way to the sea. New Jersey benefits from its waters nearer the mouth as much as Delaware itself. Delaware Bay has some charming little beach resorts, used by families who go there year after year. Just a little inland is the State Capital, Dover, with less than 18,000 people. It was made capital of the revolutionary area, a declared Republican State ten years before it was officially one, in 1777. The State House is a pretty country mansion in pink, topped by a cupola with a small white marble dome and weather vane.

Many millions of people pass through Delaware every year, many of them scarcely looking up from their papers. The AMTRAK main line from New York to Washington goes right through with a half-hour train service including the fastest Metroliners, but all stop at Wilmington, the State's chief port and manufacturing centre, with nearly 100,000 population.

Maryland

Next door to Pennsylvania and Delaware is the delightful State of Maryland – the Old Line State – some 10,500 square miles of 'America in Miniature'. It is 42nd in size but contains so much history and tranquil beauty it is among the top ten in America for visiting enjoyment.

It was in 1814, when watching the Stars and Stripes still fluttering in the breeze above Fort McHenry at Baltimore after a night of bombardment by British naval vessels, that Francis Scott Key wrote the "Star

Spangled Banner". This became the official National Anthem of the United States by decree of Congress in 1931. Another Marylander, James Ryder Randall, wrote a song which arouses regional emotions and became the State Anthem, the lovely melody "Maryland, my Maryland".

Captain John Smith from England first explored the territory up Chesapeake Bay in 1608, and a trading post was established in 1631 on Kent Island by William Claiborne. But the first real settlers came in 1634, sailing from England in two ships, "Dove" and "Arc", to reach St Mary's in South Maryland. There were 200 of them, mostly Catholics escaping persecution back home, and they were sent by a Mr Calvert who became Lord Baltimore. The Colony was named after Queen Henrietta Maria, wife of Charles I. No currency was used in the colony for 60 years, only locally grown tobacco.

In recent years, St Mary's has been reconstructed in the style of Plimoth Plantation in Massachusetts, with authentic buildings and workers 'caught in a time warp'. The "Dove" is cruising the indented bays of the region, a fine replica. This is a tourist area very well worth visiting, and spotlights the founding of a region between the Jamestown colonists of Virginia and the Puritans of New England.

Baltimore

At the head of Chesapeake Bay lies Baltimore on the Patapsco River, surely the most transformed city in the United States. Only 20 years ago it was called "The Drain on the Patapsco", and it was claimed that the series of tunnels which took the former Pennsylvania main line through Baltimore were built so that travellers would not have to look out at the place.

Today it is a splendid city, clean and modern and high rise, with a restored Inner Harbour which is the envy of most of the world and being copied in many lands. There are excellent buildings surrounding the inner harbour waters, among them an amazing Aquarium, while the proud USS "Constellation" of 1797 floats at a quay.

Look for a brand new hotel on the wharf of Pier Five, the "Clarion Inn", and take the diesel trolleys which maintain services (for a mere 25 cents) from uptown and other parts of Baltimore. An underground Metro now runs up Charles Street, soon to be extended, while the most modern bus classes in USA, fully air-conditioned, serve the city and suburbs. Baltimore has been declared the "most livable City in the East". This is in no small measure due to former Mayor William Schaefer, who is currently (1990–92) Governor of the State of Maryland.

Baltimore is a railroad town essentially, headquarters of the first commercial railway in America, the Baltimore and Ohio of 1829. Its triumphs, experiments and even set-backs are contained in the finest railway museum in the East, at Poppleton and Pratt Streets, its beautiful roundhouse full of genuine exhibits over a century and its wide forecourts full of real trains. The B & O Museum is open Wednesday to Sunday, administered by world-acclaimed curator John Hankey. The station site, Mount Clare, dates from 1851.

Baltimore has two dozen museums of various kinds from art to sewage (the latter is not a joke – the Public Works Museum on Eastern Avenue shows what goes on underneath). The city was first in the Western Hemisphere with gas lighting, in 1816.

Other Maryland

Capital of Maryland is charming Annapolis, site of the US Naval Academy, founded in 1835 (John Paul Jones is buried under a sarcophagus in the vaults). It may be visited free of charge. The small Capitol Building has the only wooden dome in America, built of cypress staves, and is original. This was once Capital of the United States, for one year (1783–84), and it was here that General George Washington resigned his commission to take on the presidency. The city devised by a French architect and named after him nearly did not materialise – a small town in Western Maryland called Williamsport tried to talk General Washington into letting it become the capital of the fledgling United States.

They have conducted tours of old Annapolis, guided by ladies in revolutionary costumes, which can at times be slightly embarrassing especially in the halls of the Naval Academy. My most embarrassing experience was in 1980, guided by ladies to the Sunday auctions beside the shell fish harbour. One item on offer was a bid for breakfast next morning with the Mayor (apparently unpopular then). As no one put in a bid I offered 50 cents and won! That resulted in Eggs Benedict and coffee in the historic 200 year old Maryland Inn, which prods into Church Circle like the prow of a big ship. I did get to meet Paul Theroux's brother, then a State Official, who came to breakfast with the Mayor.

Maryland has a major resort on the breezy Atlantic, called Ocean City, serving as a lung at weekends for Baltimore and Washington trippers. The State had legal gambling until

1965, and must now earn revenue from tourism, unlike its more northerly neighbour in New Jersey, where Atlantic City thrives on gaming.

Three sides of the District of Columbia in which Washington nestles is Maryland territory. The Federal Capital's amazingly good Metro system prods deep into Maryland, serving Silver Springs and Wheaton (a fine old trolley museum is located here).

Heading West, Frederick is an historic city noted for its antiques, the nearby New Market having over 100 antique shops in a row. Another 22 miles brings the driver on Highway 70 West to Hagerstown, once known as the "Hub City" where four railway systems came together. They are working on the restoration of the huge classic roundhouse and repair shops, together with the world's largest turntable, which when complete will create a "Williamsburg of Railroading" deep in the heart of Maryland.

Only a dozen miles from Hagerstown is the site of Antietam Battlefield, where the bloodiest Civil War battle took place during the Confederates first invasion of the North. Casualties on that one day, September 17, 1862, were the worst recorded in war until the 1916 Battle of the Somme. No less than 23,010 men fell at Antietam (sometimes called the Battle of Sharpsburg) but it resulted in a stand-off situation, although the Southerners retreated later. Antietam was a turning point in that Britain, which was about to recognise the South, withdrew in time from what would have been a fatal political move.

West of Hagerstown, deep into the high forested mountains, lies Cumberland, where road, rail, and river squeeze through a gap. A splendidly restored section of the Western Maryland Railroad carries passengers behind ex-Canadian Pacific steam locomotives for 17½ miles uphill to Frostberg. Called the Allegany Central, it runs twice daily in summer.

Highest point in Maryland is Backbone Mountain, in Garrett County, close to the West Virginia border, rising to 3,360 feet. It is a mountain lost among others of almost equal height and beauty.

There is a place only 50 miles from Washington where the Potomac and Shenandoah Rivers come together at a meeting of three States (Maryland, West Virginia, and Virginia). It is Harper's Ferry, where John Brown led his raid on the armoury in 1859, to be subsequently captured and hanged by Virginians.

John Brown was a Puritan abolitionist, and his raid with 18 supporters was a marker on the road to the final outbreak of the War Between the States. On that same Potomac, or at least on Antietam Creek leading off it, the worst battle in Maryland took place in 1862, close to the town of Sharpsburg. It is now the Antietam National Battlefield.

West Virginia
West Virginia is a State in its own right, brought about by breaking away from Virginia at the time of the Civil War after disagreement about rule from Richmond and various policies. It fought on the Union side in that War as the new State of Kanawha, but changed its name to West Virginia after joining the Union in 1863.

It is best known for its abundant coal mining, but it is also very scenic with plenty of mountains and the Allegheny Plateau. Capital of the 24,000 square mile State is Charleston, with about 85,000 people, by a small margin the largest city in the State. The capitol building is very large, built as late as 1932 on the banks of the Kanawha River, in whose waters its splendid golden dome is reflected.

Virginia

Richmond, capital of Virginia and of the Confederacy, from 1861–65 so strangely close to Washington, is an interesting place to visit not only for Civil War buffs. Only 115 miles from the Federal Capital and served in two hours by half a dozen trains a day, and in little more than two hours by several coach line operations, it is on the way to Colonial Williamsburg, without doubt the finest open air museum in the world.

More than 220,000 people live in Richmond, with another 300,000 in the suburbs. The old terminal station in Broad Street has been pulled down, and AMTRAK trains stop at a new one well outside the city, but this is a through station allowing faster services to the South and East, while a shuttle bus meets all trains. The most notable feature of the city is the Capitol building, said to have been wholly designed by Thomas Jefferson in the style of Maison Carrée in Nimes, France. It is one of the eleven capitols without a dome, but is nonetheless very imposing, dominating Capitol Square.

On the way to Richmond the Rappahannock River will have been crossed and the city of Fredericksburg passed through, seen almost in its entirety from the train window. A long and terrible siege by Union forces was finally successful after a major battle in late 1864, which eventually led to the fall of Richmond itself. There are major military installations and fort areas between the Potomac at Washington and the James River on which Richmond stands, notably the huge Quantico Marine Reservation and the A. P. Hill US Army Reservation, legacies of the years of build-up during the Civil War.

Williamsburg is 56 miles East-South-East of Richmond, a faithful reconstruction of the old colonial town begun in 1926 and still not completely finished. It is authentic in every detail (like the smaller Plimoth Plantation in Massachusetts) with craftsmen at work and shops open for business as they were in the 18th century, selling goods from that period. Some 400 restored buildings and 100,000 artefacts are there, with horses and carriages and wagons – the only contemporary things admitted are tourists with their cameras.

Norfolk as a major naval base and Newport Mews as a merchant port are both interesting, particularly for the sight of the s.s. "United States", once the great Blue Ribband holder on the Atlantic, which has been lying at buoys, sadly rotting, for the past 18 years. To cross from Norfolk to Newport Mews there is a unique bridge-tunnel several miles long. An even longer version crosses Chesapeake Bay to Cape Charles. Virginia's seagirt shores are notable for great bridges, and so are its rivers, the one over the James River being worthy of mention.

Washington D.C.

Turning now to Washington D.C., the city nearly all American and foreign visitors want to visit, it is highly appropriate to utter a few words of warning. This is not the beautiful and relatively small capital many of us knew from forty years ago, and some knew from its wartime importance when, from 1942 to 1945, it was the driving and funding force of the effort to overturn the Nazis and Japanese. Although confined to its District of Columbia which used to be 100 square miles and is now only 67 (the rest was given back to Virginia), it has expanded in all directions and its population, about 200,000 in immediate pre-war days, has swelled to 637,000 within D.C. and to nearly three millions in Greater Washington taking in the Virginia and Maryland suburbs.

Two out of every three residents are black, the highest proportion of any big city in America. Drugs and gangland fighting are very evident and the city's murder rate is the highest in the land. In some, indeed many, areas, Washington can be dangerous, especially at night. One should not be on foot after dark, but the magnificent subway system is reckoned safe and so are central bus routes. This is not a city to drive in unless one has some knowledge of the circles and avenues arising from Pierre L'Enfant's grand design. But taxis are relatively cheap; the city is divided into four zones for taxi rides, and one zone costs little more than a bus or subway at peak periods. Crossing a zone adds at least a Dollar, while entering Virginia or Maryland (and to enter Virginia it is only necessary to drive across the Potomac bridges) can double or treble costs.

No building in Washington may stand higher than the Washington Monument, reflecting in the pool of the Mall. The Monument, of white Maryland marble, stands 555 feet, so there is no highrise in the city, but some buildings are vast. The Pentagon is the biggest in the World, while the Treasury and Commerce buildings, only a few storeys high, spread over larger areas than had ever been used for individual buildings prior to the Pentagon (which, in any case, is over the Potomac near Foggy Bottom).

Books and pamphlets galore will list and describe the important places to see in the city, the Lincoln Memorial a must for most people. There are more pillars and columns than in Rome, and even as recently as the late 1970's craftsmen could still be found to carve the marble for the Raeburn Building. The streets, faithfully following L'Enfant's masterplan, are 100 or 110 feet wide, while the great avenues are 400 feet wide and a mile long (there are exceptions). The streets are mostly numbered and the avenues named after States. The circles where streets and avenues collide bear the names of famous Americans.

The finest museum complex in the world, the Smithsonian, should be given half a day of any visitor's time. The big new thing is Space, with relevant exhibits and a marvellous film (tickets, free, needed). The Aircraft section has the restored original of the Wright Brothers and the "Spirit of St Louis" of Colonel Lindbergh. Among the trains, the beautiful Southern Railway Pacific locomotive from 1926, with an audio sounding beside it to reproduce the action with the engine leaving Atlanta on an express, has been a firm favourite for years. Just one other new exhibit to point out and that is a Huber giant farm steam traction engine, recently restored and given to the Smithsonian by a friend of mine.

Cherry blossom time sees Washington at its best and this means the April to May period. Most parts of the United States are at their climatic and visual best during the Fall (certainly mid September to mid October) but Washington has the freshness and colour of spring to enjoy. Summer is such an exhaustingly humid time in and around the Federal Capital that there is no sudden relaxation with temperature drop in September.

Every visitor can and usually does visit the Capitol, and this means 14 million people a year. It is free and guided, but it may be necessary to await a tour, perhaps for up to two hours at busy times. The guides are mistresses of their art and make the life of the building, particularly the vital chambers, come alive. Although security is tight these days, there are still free tours of the White House most mornings from 10 am to noon. Tourists line up at booths on the Ellipse (just South of the White House) for tickets, and there is seating while waiting. During the winter this ticket office is closed and visitors simply line up at the East Gate under watchful scrutiny and are then taken through. Only the ground floor public rooms are shown.

Now fully restored, the enormous Union Station at the foot of Capitol Hill has the finest overall roof of any building in Washington. It has acres and acres of beautiful flooring and contributes its share of columns to Washington's total. The facilities inside, including train services, are the best of any terminal in the United States (although the lower level of Union Station is not a terminal but carries through tracks to the South).

Finally Mount Vernon – the most visited of America's shrines – is a must for Americans and interesting for those from overseas. It lies 16 miles South of Washington on a hill overlooking the Potomac. George Washington lived here from 1754 to his death in 1799. No guides are there but one can go by Metrobus any time in the day. Best way is by boat – Washington Boat Lines cruise it in an hour.

CANADA

Voyageurs
National Park

MINNESOTA

Duluth

Isle Royale National Park

Sault Ste. Marie

MICHIGAN

WISCONSIN

Mackinaw City

Mackinac Island

Minneapolis • Eau Claire

St. Paul •

La Crosse

Green Bay

MICHIGAN

Rochester •

Baraboo

• Grand Rapids

Detroit

IOWA

• Milwaukee

Madison

Lansing •

• Sioux City

Cedar Rapids

Indiana Dunes National Seashore

Dearborn •

Cleveland

Amana •

Chicago •

Des Moines •

Iowa City

South
Bend

Toledo

• Akron

Council Bluffs

OHIO

Millersburg

Peoria

INDIANA

St. Joseph

Hannibal

ILLINOIS

Fort Wayne •

Dayton

• Columbus

Independence

Springfield

Indianapolis •

• Cincinnati

Kansas City

St. Louis •

Terre
Haute

Louisville •

• Frankfort

KANSAS

Jefferson City

Shawnee
National
Forest

• Lexington

MISSOURI

KENTUCKY

Paducah

• Springfield

Mammoth Cave
National Park

Cumberland Gap
National Historic Park

TENNESSEE

ARKANSAS

• Fort Smith

OKLAHOMA

Little Rock

MISSISSIPPI

Pine Bluff •

CENTRAL WEST

TEXAS

Hot Springs
National Park

*including
Chicago*

LOUISIANA

40

4.   Central West including Chicago

Ohio, Indiana, Kentucky, Illinois, Michigan, Missouri, Minnesota, Iowa, Arkansas, Wisconsin

Ohio

Settlers did not attempt to push westwards over the barrier of the Allegheny Mountains until after the original Thirteen Colonies had declared independence, and even then it was spasmodic. Exceptions were those who took to canoes and followed the early French fur traders around the top of New York State and into the Great Lakes. Strong land parties began around 1793, however.

There were huge tracts of forest and fertile land and some wide open spaces in what is now Ohio and Indiana. There were Indians, not as many nor as determined to hold their land, as were to be encountered later on treks further West. The war between the United States and Great Britain from 1812 to 1814 had a decided effect, for the Indians had allied themselves with the British and were shattered in a major battle in October 1813 which made all lands out to and including Detroit safe for American settlers. That war, incidentally, is regarded as a draw and ended with the peace treaty signed at Ghent in December 1814.

The first organised settlement in what became the State of Ohio was at Marietta in 1788, and a few later ones were founded but greatly harassed by Indians until Anthony Wayne led an armed party against them and won decisively at the Battle of Fallen Timbers in 1794. Only nine years later, Ohio was declared a State and entered the Union, the 17th to do so.

What changed the pioneers into settlers was in reality rail access, available from the conquest of the Allenghenies by the Horseshoe Curve (described in Chapter Three). They poured in, from Germany, England, Poland and Italy; they cleared the dense forests (but not entirely – Ohio still has some six million acres of forest); they raised crops, but above all they founded cities which manufactured things, items much in demand then as they still are. No one city dominates the State; there are, in fact, ten with big populations and prosperous output.

The Capital is Columbus, on the Ohio River, chosen as a location because it is more or less in the centre. This is the site of Ohio State University, one of the biggest in the nation. On the shore of Lake Erie, Cleveland is the biggest city, with nearly 800,000 people, but Cincinnati, in the Southwest corner of the State, has over half a million, while Columbus is growing and has reached 550,000. Toledo, at the extreme end of Lake Erie, musters more than 375,000 while Dayton is over quarter of a million. It is a good spread of big cities but they still need fast transport.

Back in 1979 there was a well thought-out project called ORTA (Ohio Rapid Transit Authority) which set out to link all the big cities with high speed trains. I was involved in the early stages and went around lecturing on it. But funding seems to have held it up, and Ohio still depends on cars, or infrequent air links and buses. All the AMTRAK National Railroad Corporation lines pass through Ohio on an East–West basis; what is still desperately needed is a North–South system.

What should a tourist go to Ohio for? Business travellers go there and spread widely but that is different. However, there is one city which has powerful international attractions and that is Dayton. Here they stage an annual Air Show which must be the biggest in the world by a long chalk. It is held over a weekend in summer. The Air Force museum exhibits 160 historic aircraft, open, free, all year and there is also an Aviation Hall of Fame. The reason is that Dayton is considered the birthplace of aviation, because two brothers who had a bicycle shop in town made early flying machines which they took, laboriously, overland to the Outer Banks of North Carolina and where, in December 1903, they flew the first heavier-than-air powered aeroplane. They were the Wrights, and their bicycle shop is a National Shrine. Orville Wright lived to see jets in action, dying in 1948 at the age of 77.

Indiana

To the immediate West of Ohio is Indiana, slightly smaller but of similar appearance. It was admitted as a State in 1816 five years after General Harrison defeated Tecumseh, famed Indian leader of a native confederation, at the Battle of Tippecanoe. Indianapolis is by far the biggest city, with nearly 800,000 people, and is also the State Capital. It is the site of the main reason why international visitors flock to Indiana – to see the great 'Indy' car race. The Indianapolis 500 is held on one day a year on banked track, and is one of the fastest and most spectacular – and also most dangerous – races in the world. Charter flights are arranged from England, Italy and Germany.

Kentucky

Bordering both Indiana and Ohio to the South is the Blue Grass State of Kentucky, rolling away westwards from the mountains into glorious grassy plains. Daniel Boone was the man of history who blazed the trail to Kentucky through the Cumberland Gap to found Boonesville in 1775, and the State was admitted in 1792 as the 15th in the Union. The comparatively small city of Frankfort is the State Capital, one of the smallest capitals in America with less than 25,000 people, but it boasts a beautifully balanced Capitol building with a lovely copper dome.

If Ohio brings in aviation fans and Indiana the car racing addicts, Kentucky attracts horse people. It was recognised very early on that the magnificent grasslands would make glorious paddocks for horse breeding. The Kentucky Derby is staged at Louisville every spring, over 1¼ miles, modelled on the English Derby but even richer. The Bluegrass Stakes are held in spring over a 15 day period at Lexington. The Red Mile takes place several times a year, on a clay track, at Lexington. HM the Queen visits Kentucky from time to time on a private basis, seeing and buying horses. Do go to the Kentucky Horse Park at Lexington.

Although Kentucky is synonymous

with 'Colonels' and Mint Juleps, it was on the side of the North during the Civil War. Slaves were never a significant part of its economy. There is a Southern accent to be heard and savoured, and most inhabitants are strikingly courteous. Abraham Lincoln was born in Kentucky at Hodgenville. 'My Old Kentucky Home', by the way, is at Bardstown.

In what is called the Purchase Country in the Southwest of Kentucky the massive Ohio River – which has flowed down through Paducah where the Tennessee River joins – meets the Mississippi at Cairo (pronounced Kayrow) Point. Bridges enable one to reach Fort Defiance State Park at the confluence and to watch the busy river traffic. Here one will see pusher tugs shoving hard at barges carrying up to 200,000 tons of merchandise. They may make only a mile in an hour, but this means 'goods on the go' serving America's heartland. This Purchase region is very fertile indeed, well watered and productive of all kinds of livestock and crops. It contrasts with Central Kentucky's horse-breeding and Eastern Kentucky's prolific coal mining; Ashland is an important coal city.

Illinois
Cairo and Fort Defiance are not in Kentucky. Once the bridge over the Ohio has been crossed the State becomes Illinois, at its southern extremity. Illinois calls itself with reason the 'Inland Empire', a long State extending 390 miles (and 210 miles across), down from windy Chicago on Lake Michigan to the Southern flavour of Cairo. The first settlers came by water in about 1720 but it was virtually 100 years before the population grew enough for Illinois to be admitted as the 21st State of the Union.

In keeping with the main policy of having a capital in the middle of the State and not the biggest city (there are several exceptions), Springfield has that honour. It is 185 miles South of Chicago with what for the Mid-West is a good train service. One train is named "The State House", another "Abraham Lincoln", and they take about 3½ hours.

Chicago
Still the Second City of America, Chicago is a big working metropolis spread around the southern shores of Lake Michigan. About three million people live within its limits, but another four and a half million live in its suburbs, which go out to the edge of Indiana and of course deep into Illinois. The suburbs of Chicago are the most pronounced in all North America, and it is reckoned that 15 percent of Americans live within a 200 mile radius of a circle drawn with Chicago at its centre. Even at that, about a third of that circle would be 'lost' in Lake Michigan.

They call Chicago 'World Capital of Railroads', the world in this sense – as indeed it is all over the United States where this dramatic claim is made – meaning America-wide. In some cases it is simply State wide, like 'World Capital of Catfish' down South. A neighbouring State will have a town or lake making a similar claim.

However, with the railway system, Chicago is definitely leader in North America, probably in the Western Hemisphere. This build-up of railroads began relatively late. All early settlers came to Chicago by water, using the Great Lakes plus portages, and those from the East came by rail to the track-end and then by Erie Canal. Only very few prior to 1837, when the place was recognised as a sound

43

permanent settlement, struggled overland. The Indians, who lived in and around it, called the place Checagou, which means powerful-smelling wild onion.

By 1840, Chicago had a population of about 5,500 people, but as yet no trains (the Eastern States had several thousand miles of track by then). By 1850, however, Chicago had rails and the Chicago and Alton Railroad was almost completed while links to the East were completed by 1851. After that growth was rapid. Eventually, Chicago had six terminal stations for passenger trains and an assortment of interconnected freight yards. Passengers between East and West had to change stations in Chicago and the famous millionaire Huntington Hartford made a renowned statement "a hog can cross the Continent but a man cannot". The situation did not alter until the coming of AMTRAK, America's National Railroad Passenger Corporation, in 1971, when all trains ran into the giant Union Station (completed in 1926) except for suburban services. Santa Fe's Dearborn Terminal, Baltimore and Ohio's Grand Central, New York Central's La Salle Street, and Illinois Central's terminal have all been torn down and replaced by highrise urban development. As for freight, at its height the Chicago freightyards handled 23 million tons daily.

The city was into the aviation scene quite early on and Chicago Midway handled more aircraft movements in 1939 than any other airport in the world. The mantle passed after the war to Chicago O'Hare, and until very recently overtaken by Atlanta this remained the busiest for movements of all kinds in the world (London is the busiest from a purely international aspect).

Chicago has excellent public transport, with a subway system (linking the Airport with Downtown), an elevated railway describing a loop which has given its name to the Loop enclosing the city's business district, and extensive bus lines, many of the vehicles being Swedish or German articulateds. Downtown is too busy for on-street car parking, but there are some very costly multiple-storey parking places. A nice touch in transport for those feeling rich is the horse and carriage ride in the Water Tower area. Most are based outside the Drake, one of Hilton Vista's finest.

Poland contributed most to Chicago's ethnic background. It is reckoned to be a bigger Polish city than any except Warsaw. Italy, Sweden and Germany have contributed, too, and Ireland is represented though not on the scale found in Boston and New York. Hard work is a feature of the place, and they are still slightly self-conscious about the gangsterism of 1920–33, led by Italians and Sicilians. Incidentally, Chicago got extremely tough with the gangs at the end and forcibly deported them to the Twin Cities (Minneapolis and St Paul) 400 miles away.

If time is limited on a visit to the Second City, one place not to be missed is the Museum of Science and Industry, on the southern lakeshore at 57th Street close by the electric train stop (Illinois Central Lines). Outside is a captured German U-boat, intact. Also outside is the first diesel transcontinental train, the "Burlington Zephyr" of 1936. Inside it is a wonderland, world famous for its 'walk-through' human heart, and the coal mine complete with functioning machinery nearby. Entry to this amazing museum is free, as it is to the Chicago Academy of Sciences on the North side at Lincoln Park.

Trains leave Union station for all parts of the United States served by AMTRAK, and also Toronto in Canada (a daytime ride). Aircraft also leave O'Hare for all parts, and the city is a hub for long distance buses of the Greyhound system.

Michigan

The great State of Michigan across the Lake to the East of Chicago, is in many ways Chicago's lung. All of the long coastline facing Lake Michigan is beach and resort, holiday home and forest. This is the State where Kalamazoo is located, a real city where they make paper. Songs have been written about it but perhaps most praise is due to the fact that Kalamazoo was the first metropolitan area to close its downtown streets and turn them into pedestrian precincts. That was in 1959, and it did not entirely please Michigan's largest city, the one they call 'Mo-town', Detroit, in the Southeast corner.

The capital of Michigan is the pleasant small city of Lansing, set roughly in the middle of the main part of the State. It became capital in 1837 but was founded, although not named as such, by French missionaries 160 years before that. Trappers came, too, and stretched their lines up to 100 miles to catch the abundant fur-bearing animals. There are still more bear and wolverine in Michigan, especially the Upper Peninsular, than anywhere else East of the Mississippi.

Shipping is important to Chicago with vessels on the Great Lakes and after the opening of the St Lawrence Seaway with freighters coming from the ocean. The waterfront and harbour remain busy but much of the freight these days is handled by barges towed across Lake Michigan. It is worth mentioning that the five Great Lakes (and Michigan is the second largest) can be extremely rough and dangerous from short, steep fresh water waves during bad weather. Chicago is known as the Windy City for good reasons – wild gales can burst in from the lake throughout the year. Even in July I have known a Sunday with hot sun and a shade temperature of 88 degrees give way on the Monday to a screaming northerly down from Canada forcing out overcoats and making breath steam from people walking along Michigan Boulevard.

In good weather one of the pleasantest things to do in Chicago is to take a boat trip through the city's canals under all the 50 bridges then out into the Harbour for a short lake cruise. This shows a lot of the buildings, which have always been in the forefront of architecture for this was the home of Frank Lloyd Wright (although his work was mainly in the suburbs), William Holabird (City Hall), James Gamble Rogers, and Louis Sullivan (Chicago Auditorium). The tallest building in the world for many years was the Sears Tower, 110 storeys, near Union Station, with a wonderful viewing gallery on the 103rd floor, but this has now been overtaken by New York City's World Trade Center. Another tall building with good viewing is 'Big John', the John Hancock Center, on Michigan Avenue at Delaware Street, the fifth in the world, with vistas northwards and out across the lake.

The reason good architecture developed in Chicago is that a fire in 1871, caused by a cow which knocked over an oil lamp, destroyed the entire city apart from one structure, the Water Tower. This solitary survivor is on Michigan Avenue at Chicago Avenue, serving as a museum and visitor center, clearly a place any tourist should call at soon after arrival in the city to get the abundant maps and pamphlets on the various attractions. These include one of the world's great orchestras, the Chicago Philharmonic and an annual two day event called Ravinia Festival, an outdoor music feast (with lawn picnics) held at the end of June on the North Shore.

Along that North Shore fronting Lake Michigan are the great homes of wealthy Chicagoans, seen at their finest in elegant suburbs such as Highland Park and Winnetka. The latter was famed in song by "Big Noise from Winnetka", and indeed one needs to be a 'big noise' to afford the type of residence one sees in the green and wooded suburb. This area is served by double-decker trains of the Chicago and North Western Railway, which are well supported by the stockbrokers and other business people going to the city. Chicago is the greatest grain market, also for livestock.

Detroit

Detroit is massive, vital for business travellers in the automotive industry. Tourists interested in cars (and planes) will find a visit to the great Henry Ford Museum in Dearborn (a Detroit suburb) and the Henry Ford Foundation's Greenfield Village (a reconstruction of a typical just pre-car American village of the late 19th Century) absolutely fascinating.

Detroit can be rough and dangerous in some areas. Best is the restored waterfront zone where intense Great Lakes shipping traffic can be seen on the St Clair River which links Lake Erie to Lake St Clair and Lake Huron. Canada's Windsor is directly across the water, spanned by the Ambassador Bridge.

Missouri, St Louis, Kansas City

St Louis (always St Lewis not Louey) is a massive city at and just South of the confluence of the Missouri and Mississippi Rivers. More than 2½ million people live in its metropolitan area. It is the epitome of Mid-West America – if it goes in St Louis it will go all over mid-America. The accents are flat and distinctive, the outlook rather insular. Less than half the dwellers in this huge place have ever seen the sea. It is 5½ hours by land, 90 minutes by air, from Chicago.

French fur trapper Louis Laclede found it coming down the Mississippi and named it after his King, Louis XIV, but the exact date seems not to be known. In any case it disappeared into the maw of the Louisiana Territory and stayed that way until the Louisiana Purchase of 1803 (see Chapter 11), becoming important as the starting point for the Lewis and Clark Expedition a year later. St Louis marks Laclede's Landing, and close by rears a great arch, the Gateway Arch, an elegant structure soaring 630 feet above the waterfront. It is quite new, designed by Finnish architect Eero Saarinen, in 1966. People may take a light train, not a lift, to the top to get a fascinating view of the riverfront and the river junction. Moored on the levee are river boats. Do not miss out on a visit to "Golden Rod", the most authentic showboat in America.

St Louis owes its reputation to being a gateway to the West. So many wagon trains started from here or from St Jo some way up the Missouri. The famous Butterfield Stage started from St Louis on its 24 day journey to California, going down by way of Texas and New Mexico over a distance of 2,800 miles. It ran from 1858 until the Union Pacific–Central

Pacific trans-continental railroad opened in 1869, and in those eleven years it ran twice a week and never once failed to reach its destination. There are no recorded instances of hold-ups or Indian attacks.

Kansas City (Missouri), on the other side of Missouri 280 miles to the West, is another river junction, where the Kansas flows into the Missouri. The city, with a metropolitan population of over a million, has less history than St Louis, having been founded by yet another French trapper, but not until 1826. Always a stopover on the Way West, it grew in importance with the coming of several railroads, later boasting the most monumental non-terminal station in the United States – which is still there but used by a mere four AMTRAK trains a day. In 1936 it had 300 passenger trains daily using 28 tracks. It is the regional capital of hard-wheat country, while its stockyards are among the Big Four of the nation.

Unlike St Louis, where the buses are good, Kansas City has poor public transportation, and even the airport (a long way out of town) has only spasmodic links, and expensive ones at that. If you need to go into town and there are two or more in the party, rent a car – you need it around town and you actually save money just on the return trip to the airport, especially at weekends when buses are appallingly scarce.

Minnesota, Iowa, Missouri, Arkansas, Wisconsin

Mid-America capitals run more or less in a straight line North to South, from St Paul of Minnesota, through Des Moines, Iowa, Jefferson City of Missouri to Little Rock, capital of Arkansas. Of these, St Paul on the headwaters of the Mississippi and the limit of navigation for bigger vessels, is highest on the list for a visit. The imposing capitol building with its big dome is one of the best in the nation. It was named in 1841, having been discovered earlier by a curious settler-explorer called 'Pig's Eye' Parrant. The city is noted for medical facilities, the nearby Mayo Clinic attracting patients from all over the world. Because of the severe winter climate, when 40 below zero Fahrenheit is not unknown, there is a vast enclosed shopping area, linked by warmed bridges across city streets. This was the first of its kind, now copied although not exceeded, by other cities for various reasons, some to provide air-cooled malls to beat the heat.

Minnesota is a huge State, of 84,000 square miles, big enough to be part Great Lakes territory, part Great Plains, and part wheatlands of Mid-America. The northern half consists of rocky ridges, forests and deep lakes – just how many lakes no one has certain knowledge but including ponds the total runs into many thousands. The official title is 'Land of Ten Thousand Lakes' but the State Government counted 12,034 exceeding ten acres in size back in 1980. Often uninhabited, some lakes are home to just one family for a summer vacation. This is Minnehaha Country, the Land of Longfellow. The largest city is Minneapolis, the Twin of St Paul, and they are now grown together, thus earning the title "Twin Cities".

Des Moines, Iowa, founded as a fort in 1843, is at the junction of the Des Moines and Raccoon rivers. Business travellers go there because it is second only to Hartford, Connecticut, as an insurance company headquarters, and also because Massey-Ferguson has its North American plant there. As yet

47

there is no strong appeal to overseas tourists but there are plenty of cultural and fun activities.

Missouri's capital, Jefferson City, in the centre of the State, is a medium sized, well laid out place founded in 1735. It has the Museum of the Plains Indian. Not in the city but contributing to Missouri's attractions are the Mark Twain State Park at Florida, statues to Tom Sawyer and Huckleberry Finn, and the Pony Express Museum at St Joseph on the river (this legendary endeavour, involving rapid comunication from the Mississippi–Missouri area to California, lasted less than 18 months but is a fundamental part of American history). Gary Cooper was born in Missouri.

Little Rock, on the Arkansas (this is pronounced 'Arkansaw'), was settled very early on, in 1686, and has developed into the largest city in the State, as well as being capital. It is not a tourist city, but the State has Hot Springs, some of the best and most widely sought for curative purposes, and is noted for the Crater of Diamonds near Murfreesboro, the only diamond mine in USA. Arkansas was on the Union side in the Civil War.

One other State capital in this region of mid-America is worthy of mention. This is Madison, Wisconsin, an elegant city on a big lake, dominated by the handsome domed capitol. The University of Wisconsin with 39,000 students, a strongly Germanic centre of learning, has its campus in the city area, and its famous well-supported American football fields.

5.   The Southeast and Florida

Florida, Georgia, South Carolina, North Carolina

Background

From Chesapeake Bay to the southern tip of Florida the emphasis is on water and beaches, sand and sunshine. The climate is officially Warm Temperate, merging into Sub Tropical in Florida, but even Key West, the southernmost community on mainland America, misses being in the real tropics by some 60 miles. The States in question are North Carolina, South Carolina, Georgia, and Florida. Each have their differences, sometimes quite distinctive.

Many years before the Pilgrim Fathers arrived on the shores of New England, settlers from England forged two colonies in the South East, one on Roanoke Island in what is now North Carolina, the other at Jamestown in nearby Virginia. The first disappeared without trace in late Elizabethan times, the second survived and prospered. But the very first European settlement in America was at St Augustine in Florida, when Ponce de Leon came from Spain and surveyed the coast, in 1513, leading to a permanent settlement in 1565.

Growing tobacco, learned from the indigenous Indians, became the important crop of North Carolina, called Virginia in the early days, and it remains so despite the present harassment of the 30 to 40 percent of people who smoke. Cotton was imported and planted in ideal conditions, soon becoming a rich export. But these crops needed labour, and in the extreme summer heat coupled with high summer humidity, the settlers opted for slaves. Several millions were brought, usually under appalling conditions, from the West Coast of Africa, and this state of affairs continued for 250 years, a major slice of American history.

After the American War of Independence, the original British Colonies became States, thirteen of them ending at the Florida border with Georgia. Following the success of the Louisiana Purchase (see chapter 11), fledgling America decided to try and buy Florida from Spain. In 1819, Washington succeeded after a great deal of bargaining, and got the whole Florida Peninsula for five million Dollars under the Adams–Onis Treaty, relatively costly at 60 Dollars per square mile.

Florida

Discounting all the gold that was retrieved from Alaska, Florida must have proved the best bargain. An apparently worthless sand-spit hundreds of miles long has been transformed into the World's playground, at first in winter and now in summer. Apart from countless American 'snowbirds' who flock to Florida to escape the northern cold, it attracts more than a million British visitors a year and is now as important a 'package holiday' destination for Europeans as the Mediterranean.

Henry Flagler, the railroad builder, first put Florida on the vacation map by building his East Coast Railroad down to Palm Beach in the late 1890's. The rich and famous wintered there at great luxury hotels which Flagler also constructed. Further South than Palm Beach was considered 'no go' territory, with swamps and Seminole Indians, mosquitoes and high humidity. But Julia Tuttle, an elderley widow, lived on the coast in a village called Miami, and one winter, when a cold spell had withered the Florida orange blossom down as far as Palm Springs, sent a runner to Flagler with sprigs of unaffected blossom.

Henry Flagler pushed his railroad down to Miami as quickly as possible. Ths swamps in the area were drained. The sand spit came alive, not with insects but with people. Property developers prospered and by 1910 Miami was a winter resort for the wealthy enjoying international fame. There were ups and downs, high in the Roaring Twenties, the biggest 'down' during the Depression (confounded by a dreadful hurricane in 1935 which destroyed part of the city and wiped out the Florida Keys along with Flagler's railway extension to Key West).

Today the boom extends over much of Florida, leaving parts of Miami Beach a bit seedy while the city itself is rich from housing corporate banking, more than sixty major banks being established in the high rise city. Central Florida has been transformed within twenty years thanks largely to special attractions, of which Disney World is the leader. Orlando was a sleepy town in 1968; now it is a spreading metropolis serving not only Disney World but Epcot, Universal Studios, MGM, Sea World and numerous other international attractions. Unknown to 98 percent of Europeans twenty years ago, Orlando now receives NINETY flights a week from Britain alone!

Miami and even its beach area is more Hispanic than American, with Cuban, Honduran, and Haitian immigration (both legal and illegal). This is a region of rising violence and drug abuse.

On the plus side, the newly expanded Dodge Island downtown Port area has become the "Cruise ship capital of the world". More than 40 liners are based here or at Fort Lauderdale, operating mostly on week-long cruises to the Bahamas, Caribbean, and Mexico. Several of the world's largest passenger ships come up the waterway to Dodge Island, flying the flags of Norwegian Cruise Lines, Royal Caribbean Cruises, and Carnival. None fly the stars and stripes.

Tampa was an established city on Florida's Gulf Coast, famed for cigars and oranges at the turn of the century. It is now part of a complex of cities and resorts known as the Pinellas Sun Coast stretching along some thirty miles of beach. The "Don Cesar" at St Petersburg beach is one of the original 'Pink Palace' hotels of Florida, built in 1929 and now better than ever.

So much is heard of Florida for the holidaymaker and retired person that it sounds as if the State is over-run with people and buildings, hotels (and it has hundreds of giant resort hotels built in recent years outstripping any in the world) and golf courses, spacious attractions and developed beaches. In fact, Florida is the 22nd State in size, and is twice as big in area as the whole island of Ireland, so plenty of room exists for urbanised

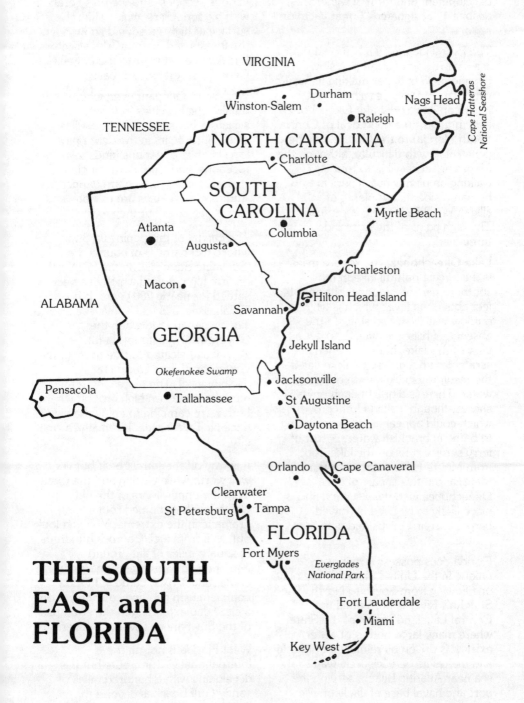

THE SOUTH EAST and FLORIDA

development and for real wilderness, despite 12 designated "Great vacation regions".

The Everglades, now a National Park, is a vast region of swamp, a slow moving ooze of water making its way very, very steadily yet almost imperceptibly from Lake Okeechobee (which takes up a good deal of Central South Florida) to the Gulf. It may be penetrated with difficulty, although the fringes are accessible to tourists walking on plankways. There are no human residents but plenty of alligators, while bird life is profuse. The high point of the Everglades is just three feet!

Lake Okeechobee, 700 square miles, is the largest natural lake in the southern part of America, but only 14 feet above sea level, which is why its outflow waters are so slow. In the absence of hills it is difficult to get a view of this lake, but even when one scrambles up a grassy bank to see it, the result is usually a vista of sludgy water. There is a quiet beach on its shores, though, called Upthegrove, which could appeal to visitors wanting to bathe in brackish water. A sort of ferry service runs on the lake, too, from Moore Haven across to Port Mayaca, but this is part of the Okeechobee waterway system and is more likely to be used by towed barges carrying citrus and pine than people.

Florida does possess a real river, unique in the United States as the only one flowing from South to North. The St John's River is born amid the Central Lakeland region of the State, where many large bodies of water exist. It is driven by rainfall not altitude and makes its very leisurely way to the sea near Atlantic Beach, serving the port and naval base of Jacksonville. On its waters there are air-boats over

various sections, strange noisy craft with big propellers, which skim the surface at high speed and show riders the forests and, particularly, alligators. It is the nearest river to the famous Cape Canaveral rocket base.

Wild life is abundant everywhere outside the big cities, not only alligators but salt water crocodiles, small black bears in the dense pine forests, deer of various kinds, raccoons, and – not surprisingly – snakes, some of which are dangerous. And rare these days are manatees, a sort of sea cow, but they exist.

The capital of this peninsula State, whose nickname is of course the 'Sunshine State', lies in the far North, on firm high ground which has been settled for nearly 200 years. It is Tallahassee, 345 feet above sea level, a site chosen in 1845 when the Governor of West Florida (at Pensacola) elected to ride to meet the Governor of East Florida (at Jacksonville). The place where they met, and it was on high ground where both were camping to enjoy the view, became Tallahassee. It remains a small city.

It is way off the tourist beat but very well worth while visiting and the view from the upper floors of the old Capitol with its domed roof is dramatic in the extreme. You just look out, as if from a cliff, across hundreds of square miles of flat ground interspersed with forests and cleared cattle ranges (yes, cattle in Florida complete with genuine cowhands), on a clear day extending to the swamps of the Suwhannee (Swanny) River.

West Florida is not on the International visitors route but it is developing with a hundred miles of sandy Gulf Beaches beyond the Apalachicola River. Panama City is jaded; Walton Beach has potential, while Pensacola and its beach are worthy. Do visit Pensacola Naval Air Station and its associated museum (free). The deep water inlet and harbour of Pensacola is a base for aircraft carriers, one of which, "Lexington", does a lot of air training, and on Sundays members of the public may put to sea for a few hours in this carrier to watch naval aircraft doing deck take-offs and landings. Apply through the Naval Air Station Commander's Office.

Just a footnote on the size of Florida for those who still think in terms of a small tropical area in the sun – to drive from Key West at the end of the chain of Keys in the South to Pensacola close to the Alabama border involves a distance of 810 miles, further than from Calais to Rome.

Before taking a look at other States in this South East part of America, a word about Florida's islands may be of interest. Just how many there are is not known for certain, because annual hurricanes have swamped some, while others have appeared as growing sand spits. But the Florida Keys run into hundreds, many inhabited, with Key Largo (where a famous Humphrey Bogart movie was made) featuring the John Pennekamp Coral Reef State Park, the first entirely under water park in the world. Islands on the Gulf side are being cautiously developed, mainly for up-market visitors, such as Sanibel and Captiva Islands, reached through Fort Myers, and Longboat Key, off Sarasota. Some islands are wild life refuges, Caladesi off the Pinellas Sun Coast and St Vincent near Apalachicola township.

Georgia
Georgia borders Florida and boasts proudly of the greatest recovery of

pride and prosperity from destruction and abject poverty compared to anywhere in America. The War Between the States was its undoing, when General Sherman made his famous march "From Atlanta to the Sea". All towns and cities were burned, and 'King Cotton' was reduced to a charred princeling.

Today, Atlanta, capital of Georgia, is the greatest metropolis of the South, a sky-scraping city of immense wealth, headquarters of the Coca-Cola Empire (and that is not meant to be funny for it is a corporation richer than a large number of countries), of Delta Airlines, and the biggest convention and hotel centre in the USA. Its International Airport, Hartsfield, has just overtaken Chicago as the busiest in terms of movements in the world. There is a saying in the South that if you want to go from Heaven to Hell you must change at Atlanta. But in fact it is possible to fly anywhere from this enormous place, to London, Brussels, Hawaii, or wherever. Only when flying from one southern city to another is it usually necessary to change in Atlanta. There are at least 20 direct flights a week from London to Atlanta. In 1996 Atlanta will be host city to the Olympic Games.

Savannah is Georgia's port, the place where the Colony began in 1732. Not much survived the Sherman march and it took years to restore what could be rebuilt. It remained shabby and poor until the years after the Second World War, but then underwent a second, more determined restoration in the late 1960's. It is a city of squares, for plenty of burned-out space was available. Some of its great ante-bellum homes look as if they had never felt Sherman's torch. There are plenty of giant live oaks in town, hung with Spanish moss, which give a rich colonial atmosphere.

With a population of only about 120,000, Savannah is to some extent a living and working museum, but it remains the pride of its inhabitants. A two mile section of the restored city has been designated a National Landmark District, but of course it has a 'strip' of fast food and motel buildings extending inland, like so many cities in the States. The small modern railway station has been built about six miles out of town, served by AMTRAK with eight trains a day. The main industry of the area is papermaking, from the abundant pine trees or palmettos – one train from New York passing through is called "The Palmetto". Visitors should call at the old 1860 railroad terminal, now turned into the Savannah Visitors Centre, where walking maps are free. This is a walking city, with nearly everything worth seeing reached on foot, but if tired, very cheap Savannah Transit Authority buses can be taken. If it is summer, do not miss a two hour cruise on the Savannah river through the harbour area from Riverfront Plaza.

Charleston

About 140 miles up the coast is a sister city to Savannah, but founded about fifty years earlier. It is Charleston, South Carolina, one of the handsomest and most popular historic cities of America. More fortunate than Savannah in that the Civil War – although it actually began in Charleston Harbour – did not destroy it, the city retains the largest collection of lived-in ante-bellum homes, i.e. pre-Civil War, apart from Natchez, Mississippi.

For years after 1865 the city lay wracked in poverty but it was intact. They say the people were "too poor to paint, too proud to whitewash" so

their houses remained in a shabby, dilapidated condition until quite recently, when restoration hit with a major campaign. Downtown Charleston stands on a peninsula between the Ashley and Cooper Rivers forming the big harbour, and this quiet unspoiled zone echoes to the clip-clop of horses still, as carriages taking tourists amble around seeing the sights.

Out in the Harbour is Fort Sumter, where the first shots (fired by the Confederates) of the War Between the States were heard, in 1861. On the other side of the Harbour is the largest and most interesting Maritime Museum in America, probably in the world, where at Patriot's Point the giant aircraft carrier USS Yorktown is moored, alongside the destroyer "Laffey", the World War II submarine "Clagamore", and the nuclear-powered merchant ship "Savannah" (her reactor taken away). Charleston's operating naval base, north of Charleston off Spruill Avenue, is also open at weekends for sight-seeing tours.

Charleston has become one of the top ten tourist places in the United States, and the 1989 hurricane which swept through in September caused nation-wide alarm as it devastated outlying islands, flooding the older part of the city. However, damage has now been repaired and the numerous festivals involving old houses continue as before. Anyone visiting Charleston should not miss the 'Magnolia by Moonlight' dinners held three times a week during the season in the dining hall of the Magnolia Plantation House. Another outstanding event, in late May, is the Spoleto Festival. Charleston's Dock Street Theatre, built in 1736, is the oldest theatre in America still functioning, but like many places in the old city, it is closed during July and August when the heat is overbearing and the humidity crippling. Myrtle Beach, all 75 miles of it, lying well to the north of the city, is the escape area then – but it is in winter, or what passes for winter this far South, that Myrtle Beach is at its busiest with Canadians, when rates are cheap and 65 degrees is bliss compared to sub zero temperatures at home.

South Carolina/North Carolina

Columbia is the capital of South Carolina, a city lying in a bowl some 150 miles inland from Charleston. The Capitol building is the most dramatic feature of the relatively small city, its walls still scarred from Yankee cannons firing during the Civil War. Anyone getting to Columbia who is interested in old newsreels should make a point of visiting the McKissick Museum of the University of South Carolina. On the first floor (ground floor in European parlance) is the Movietone News Film Library containing some 60 million feet of news film shot between 1919 and 1963. Any reel can be called up by computer and viewed free of charge.

The heat can be intense in Columbia from May to September, leading to an escape route to the hills. Going westwards about 150 miles leads to Upcountry Carolina where the Appalachian Chain, shared with North Carolina, is a land of three to four thousand foot mountains, very fast flowing streams (the Chattooga National Wild and Scenic River – filmed in the movie "Deliverance" – has exciting raft trips), and the Cherokee Foothills Scenic Highway. Cool resorts abound, and in the foothills stands the city of

Spartanburg, a place of character, in no way high-rise like ultra-modern Greenville, close by but a little lower down the slope.

This slope leading up from the sea across the rising plains to the Appalachians occurs in southern parts of Virginia plus both North and South Carolina. It is known as Piedmont Country (foothills in French but locally pronounced 'Peedmont'). Neither Georgia nor Florida have it, for the mountains swing to the South West and end up in North Alabama.

There is a great deal of difference between North and South Carolina. Not only is the former two-thirds larger than its neighbour, but it has a cooler climate and grows other crops, tobacco and peanuts being the major ones. However, it is well to the fore in manufacturing.

The two great tourist areas are the Atlantic Coast and the Great Smoky Mountains in the West. The coastline is quite unique, breezy and sandy, reaching out as the Outer Banks to Cape Hatteras, where the Gulf Stream mixes with the cold Labrador Current. Hatteras marks a climatic change. It is also the point where hurricanes sweeping up from the South recurve and usually swing out harmlessly into the Atlantic. Dominated by the tallest lighthouse in the United States, Cape Hatteras stands in the middle of a National Seashore, with a scenic drive at times so narrow that salt water on either side is only feet away from the road.

By no means easy to reach, the Outer Banks are thoroughly worth while visiting. Take the toll ferry from Cedar Island on the mainland for the 90 minute crossing of Pamlico Sound to Ocracoke Island. It is almost essential to have a car with you; public transport on the banks is paper thin.

There is an alternative ferry from Swan Quarter, further North on the mainland but perhaps more accessible to Raleigh, the capital of North Carolina. This one takes two hours to Okracoke Island. Once on the tiny island with its cluster of white wooden houses and a picturesque inn, find a small, beautifully cared-for cemetery with just four graves. This is the only British War Cemetery in America excluding those of the 1776–83 War of Independence (and those are hard to find). Okracoke marks the graves of four British navymen washed ashore in 1942 after their armed trawler was sunk by a U-boat while escorting an American coastal convoy, and the Union Jack flies over it, raised and lowered appropriately by the US Coastguard. The inscription, from Rupert Brooke, is highly applicable – "There is some corner of a foreign field . . ."

The road ends along the sand spit of Okracoke Island but a free ferry carries passengers and cars across to Hatteras Island. Then follows a forty mile drive to the Oregon inlet, where a fairly new high bridge takes the road across to Bodie Island, now pointing North West. At the northern end of Bodie lies the Cradle of Aviation, the Mecca for all aircraft enthusiasts, the Kill Devil Hills. Nearby is the village of Kitty Hawk.

Once bare sandy dunes, the hills have been planted, but the level ground below them is marked to indicate the three flights made by the Wright Brothers on December 17, 1903. A tall memorial to the Wrights stands on the highest hill, while in a large memorial building, Rangers give a dramatic talk on the events leading up to the First Flight. They stand beside a replica of the powered aircraft (the original,

restored, is in the Smithsonian in Washington). In more modern light aeroplanes you can make an inexpensive flight around the area and even land on First Flight Field.

Sir Walter Raleigh's Elizabethan colonists came through one of these inlets (probably Oregon) to land on Roanoke Island. They came in August 1587 and settled. The first white child born in America, Virginia Dare, had her birthday on August 18. It is all well documented, for a ship returned to England, with two Indians, Manteo and Wanchese. But the 115 settlers became The Lost Colony. When a ship returned to Roanoke Island in 1590 the only trace of what had been a thriving colony was a sign saying 'Croatoan'. Every year, Paul Green's moving play, "The Lost Colony", is performed at the Waterside Theatre, Manteo, on the island. It has been running to capacity audiences for over 50 years. Paul Green died in 1981 at the age of 87.

Roanoke Island is linked by bridges to the mainland and to the Outer Banks, the latter road going past Kitty Hawk then crossing a huge bridge over the Albemarle Sound. This is the way to Virginia. Anyone who smokes should stop short of the border to buy cigarettes or tobacco for once across into Virginia the price escalates. It is North Carolina, formerly known as Virginia, where the tobacco comes from and the kindly State scarcely taxes its own prime product.

If asked to comment on the most surprising city of the South East, I would say Charlotte, North Carolina. Charlotte, despite its gentle name suggesting a sleepy town, is a sparkling city in the Piedmont, massively high-rise, with commerce and banking much to the fore. Nearly one million people live within its bounds, with a lot of wealth apparent. Ten years ago, not one Briton in ten would have placed it correctly on the map; today it has a direct non-stop jet air service every day from London flown by Piedmont Airlines (or that was the founding name – it is now part of US Air).

KENTUCKY

Knoxville

Nashville • *Smoky*   Gatlinburg •
              Mountains
              National Park

MISSOURI   TENNESSEE   NORTH
                                                 CAROLINA

• Memphis   Chattanooga •

                              Russell Cave
              Huntsville •   *National Monument*

ARKANSAS   GEORGIA

              MISSISSIPPI
                              Birmingham
                              •

Shreveport   ALABAMA
•   Vicksburg
                •
Natchitoches •   Jackson   Montgomery
                     •   •

              • Natchez

LOUISIANA   Mobile •   FLORIDA
                     Biloxi •

Baton Rouge •   **THE DEEP**
                                               SOUTH
Lake Charles •   New Orleans •

6. The Deep South

Louisiana, Mississippi, Tennessee, Alabama

Background

Two English surveyors named Charles Mason and Jeremiah Dixon drew a line between the Free State of Pennsylvania and what were then the 'Slave Colonies' to the South. That was in 1767, about ten years before America became a Republic by force of arms. But the Mason and Dixon Line continued throughout American history and continues, even to this day, to play an enormous part in social conditions and outlook.

Everywhere South of the Line was called, both by word and by song, 'Dixie'. But not every State below the Line belongs to the true 'South', nor did they all fight on the side of the South – or Confederate – States during the 1861–65 Civil War. Maryland, for instance, was on the Northern side, as was Kentucky.

One cannot get further South, geographically speaking, than the sub-tropical peninsula of Florida, yet in no way can that region be considered 'Deep South'. Below the Suwannee River nine out of ten inhabitants are not natives, and 'Deep South' is essentially a state of mind and of surroundings involving live oaks, swamps, cotton, langour, humid heat, and a high proportion of black people.

Today there are black Mayors in big southern cities such as Atlanta, and black millionaires in business are numerous. This was unthinkable only 35 years ago, when it was still 'Jim Crow' country and a worse system of 'apartheid' existed than South Africa ever practiced. Schools were segregated in the State of Mississippi until the early 1960's, while public buses in Alabama, North Florida, Mississippi and Georgia had a 'Jim Crow' line drawn across the floor, behind which blacks had to stand or sit on the few wooden seats while whites up front all sat on more comfortable upholstery. All had to pay the same fare, however. This did not end finally until 1966.

That was 'Deep South' which today exists as a state of mind, the physical and visible constraints removed. There was another side to the attitudes of mind, still heard but less so nowadays, when a successful black refers to 'PWT' – a struggling dirt farmer or city down-and-out for example. The initials stand for 'Poor White Trash'. A railway timetable for 1953 in my files shows some crack trains on the Southern and Louisville and Nashville railways with accommodation notes alongside the listings:- 'Not available to blacks and poor whites'.

Those are all problems of the past and do not affect modern travellers, although they should be borne in mind. The States of the 'Deep South', which are Georgia, Mississippi, Alabama, Louisiana, Tennessee, and part of the Florida 'Panhandle', are great places for tourists, with low costs, distinctive food, wonderful spring and fall weather conditions, and welcoming, usually gracious people speaking with picturesque accents for real.

New Orleans/ Louisiana/Mississippi

The big tourist Mecca in the region is the City of New Orleans, situated where the mighty Mississippi River breaks into its delta. The open waters of the Gulf of Mexico are about 130 miles down from the busy waterfront of New Orleans, which is a magnificent port with riverside berths unaffected by tides or the need for locks. Dozens of large ships come upstream every day to trans-ship their cargoes, while a few continue on up the river to Baton Rouge, capital of Louisiana and the limit of conventional navigation. It was at Baton Rouge that the controversial governor Huey Long (1893 to his assassination in 1935) was at his most flamboyant. He built a sky-scraper State House, relegating the original – with its rare inverted dome – to a museum.

In a country which thinks roads, aircraft and freight railroads, it is too often overlooked that the Mississippi is the most important shipping artery in the world. Enormous barges pushed by powerful tugs have taken the place of historic and traditional stern-wheeler steamboats in taking raw materials and all kinds of produce to the heartland of America. Very, very slowly, pushing hard upstream, loads up to 200,000 tons move more than 2000 miles to cities such as St Paul and Cincinnati. Over the last ten years the Mississippi River system handled an *annual* average of 537 million tons of cargo.

Passenger boats still survive. In fact, two of them offer the most romantic holiday trip in America. "Delta Queen", dating from 1926, and "Mississippi Queen", built (partly in Scotland) in 1976, are the last two overnight steamboats on the river. They make cruises of various lengths, sometimes ten days from St Paul on the Upper Mississippi. When I joined "Delta Queen" 25 years ago with a British newspaper reader's group, it was in Cincinnati on the Ohio River and we steamed eight days downstream, past the Ohio–Mississippi confluence at Cairo, then to Memphis (the ancient Egyptian names were deliberately selected by settlers in the early 1800's), down to Vicksburg where one sees the relics of the great siege during the Civil War, to Natchez, Baton Rouge and New Orleans.

Time and money do not always allow such wondrous luxury as a week or more of relaxation on the big sternwheelers. There are other boats, though, day tripper ones, still with a gigantic paddle wheel thrashing away aft and a steam-blown calliope to summon passengers. "Natchez" is the finest of these, and she lives at New Orleans, a new but authentic steamship doing three hour scenic trips and dinner-plus-show evening cruises.

Other big genuine steamboats are to be found at Memphis, while the latest, the "General Jackson", plies on the Cumberland River in Tennessee. These are the modern-day equivalents of the famous southern 'Show-boats', but many of the smaller stern-wheelers seen on the Mississippi, especially those which cruise up the bayous (deep creeks), are actually diesel driven, and in some cases the giant stern-wheel is only cosmetic. "Natchez", though, built in 1977, attracts steam enthusiasts from all over the world for the length of her piston thrust which, at 24 feet, is the longest ever constructed.

Visitors can get a free harbour trip in New Orleans, simply by going down to the waterfront at the bottom of Canal Street and taking the ferry across to Algiers on the opposite shore. No charge is made for pedestrians and the 15 minute trip offers fine views of the city and its famous crescent-spread along the river bank. New Orleans is known as the "Crescent City" and the AMTRAK train from New York, Washington and Atlanta is called "The Crescent".

Living costs are quite low in the city, less than half those for food and accommodation charged in such places as New York and Philadelphia. There are central bus rides for ten cents, tram rides of considerable length on the St Charles Street line (in Perley and Thomas streetcars reminiscent of "A Street Car named Desire") for 60 cents, and telephone calls are still only 10 cents, up from five cents a few years ago.

New Orleans is the home of Jazz, the Hot Jazz of the 1912–30 period. It booms out in Jackson Square, while amid the old houses in the French Quarter with their wrought-iron balconies, Jazz Clubs feature the top musicians of the day. Traditional Creole restaurants abound in this area, serving the distinctive food of the region, and there will usually be noisy helpings of authentic Jazz to go with the meal. Jazz musicians, for reasons which are not clear, call New Orleans the "Big Easy". Try Preservation Hall any night for the 'professors of the Big Easy' pounding out their beat. It was here that Louis Armstrong was discovered, and many, many more came to fame from playing the Hall.

There is a Jazz Festival in June, when the city is hot and crowded and Ragtime plus Dixieland Jazz booms all night. But the big event of the year is Mardi Gras (Fat Tuesday), with the largest parades in America, colourful, frenetic, crowded and – although free on the streets – very expensive if a room or a meal can be obtained. The weather is usually around 65 degrees Fahrenheit and at its best during the February Carnivals.

Bourbon Street in the 'Vieux Carre', the Old Square, known as the French Quarter, carefully restored and protected, is the main stem for restaurants and night clubs. They come and go but a listing of the active ones can be seen in the daily newspapers. St Louis Street is the home of one of the finest restaurants in America and certainly the most famous in New Orleans – Antoine's. Any visitor feeling flush should enjoy one dinner here, which will prove to be an expensive but magnificent gastronomic experience.

Commonest Creole dish served in most places in Louisiana is Jambalaya, which comes in many forms but is basically varieties of sea food on a bed of rice, the 'Paella of the Gulf'. Giant shrimps (the word prawn is not used in North America) are cheap and prolific, thanks to a recent discovery that the vast rice paddies to the West of New Orleans, stretching into Texas, could also breed big shrimps and langoustines, the two crops blending happily. The largest shrimps of all are caught in deep water out in the Gulf by fleets of shrimp boats mainly operating out of small ports on the Alabama coast.

Dominating the area of New Orleans around the combined bus and train terminal is the gigantic Superdome, claimed to be the world's largest covered sports arena. The massive air-conditioned domed building seats 97,000 people, and hosts the 'Sugarbowl' classics of American football but is also the venue for some of the biggest conventions. There is a cheap and frequent city bus service from the Superdrome, transport complex and the waterfront.

On the River Road from New Orleans to the State Capital, some 70 miles up the Mississippi, stands the finest original plantation home in the Deep South. This is Houmas House, fully open to the public, serving meals to tour groups. It is below the level of the river, from which it is protected by high levees, but it is not wise to climb these dykes to get a view of the river since they are sodden and one sinks up to the knees or beyond if the river is high.

The greatest concentration of 'ante-bellum' (meaning pre-Civil War) great houses is found in Natchez, on the right bank of the Mississippi about 100 miles upstream from Baton Rouge. The river twists and turns a great deal, making it a three day passage from New Orleans, but the journey can be accomplished by road in a matter of hours. Natchez escaped destruction by the Armies of the Union and so some five hundred pre 1862 homes survived intact, many of them lived in today privately, but about thirty are open during Natchez spring and fall Pilgrimage Tours, and others can be visited by appointment. Longwood, never quite completed, is the largest octagon house in USA but Stanton Hall in the High Street is my favourite.

An historic pack-horse road known as the 'Natchez Trace' runs from the waterfront of the Mississippi town through Jackson, capital of Mississippi State, to Tupelo and then on across the Tennessee border to Nashville.

The South Chapter of the Daughters of the American Revolution met and decided the old 'Trace' should be put back as a road, and in 1938, restored as a parkway, it became part of the National Parks System. Along the Trace one sees extensive cotton fields and fertile farmlands, as well as the huge dome of Jackson's Capitol Building.

End-of-the-line Nashville has gathered world wide fame in the past thirty years as the home of Country and Western music. This is the capital city of Tennessee, its Capitol Building having a spire instead of the traditional dome. Nashville tends to be a younger persons' city, those best served being between 14 and 44; the over 45's could feel slightly uneasy with its obsessions, especially the nightlife and 'Grand Ole Opry'.

For the under 45's there are chances to attend tapings for free on the Cable TV network TNN, which goes to a nation-wide audience of over 25 millions and features most of the top stars of Country and Western. On arriving in Nashville, telephone 883.7000 and tell them you are a visitor, and if from overseas the chances of a free seat are much higher.

The Cumberland River offers delightful scenic trips, aboard the diesel stern-wheeler "Music City Queen" and the new genuine steamboat "General Jackson", completed in 1984. The river flows through the centre of 'Music City USA', but Opryland to the East is the berth for "General Jackson", which provides dinner and entertainment cruises as well as daytime trips. Nashville is very chilly in the December to February period and blazing hot in July and August.

Tennessee

The three major cities of Tennessee form a triangle with Nashville the apex and Memphis and Chattanooga the base points. Memphis is a large and sprawling city situated along the East bank of the Mississippi, world famous as the home of the 'Blues' and in more recent years as the place where Elvis Presley lived. His house is a shrine open to the public and for special events celebrating his life. Europeans as well as Americans have been known to charter planes to attend. Less well known, perhaps, but important in its field is that Memphis was the founder-city of Holiday Inns and the site of the first one built. About 16 miles from the centre is the Holiday Inn University, where senior staff from the hotels world-wide are required to graduate if seeking promotion to management. The Founder of Holiday Inns, Kemmons Wilson, is no longer connected with the business, but for 30 years he was so involved at his Memphis head office he worked all hours and usually answered the phone himself.

Chattanooga stands on the Tennessee River, put on the world map by a song written in the 1930's, and it is not perhaps surprising that the old railway station has been turned into an unusual hotel, called "Chattanooga Choo-Choo". Guests sleep in converted sleeping cars drawn up along the platforms, while the great domed station is used for dining and for lounges.

No regular passenger trains work into Chattanooga these days. It is one of the largest cities in the States, with over half a million people, not to be included in the rail network. But there is a private line, the West Tennessee Railway, which runs excursion trips over a section of the Southern Railway trackage at weekends and on holidays. Try the tunnel ride in an open car!

Dominating the city is Look Out Mountain, the view from the summit encompassing a great deal of Civil War terrain and the site of fierce battles. Chattanooga was the key city which the Union armies sought to take, and after nearly three years of bloody fighting they eventually did but lost the Battle of Chickamauga 12 miles away. Chickamauga is an Indian word meaning River of Death and it certainly was for several thousand men in one of the greatest Federal disasters of the war. Later, in November 1863, during the Battle of Look Out Mountain, Union troops dislodged Confederate General Bragg's men in what is known as the 'Battle among the Clouds'. A few days later the Battle of Chattanooga was decisive and ended Confederate hopes in the western part of the Old South.

There is a funicular railway up to Look Out Mountain but on the two occasions when I have tried to use it a car has been stuck half way up. Fortunately, the mountain can be climbed by car but only with a lengthy detour across the Georgia border and up the southern side of the ridge.

No one can get full enjoyment from a visit to the Deep South without some knowledge of and interest in the War Between the States. Battlefields are preserved and well presented without loss of dignity. In the minds of many, especially the older inhabitants, the scars of the Civil War remain despite the South's recent prosperity. Some of them still call it the "War of Northern Agression" despite the first shots at Fort Sumter in South Carolina having been fired by the Confederate forces.

Alabama

The ultimate Deep South State must be Alabama, whose capital, Montgomery, boasts the 'first White House of the Confederacy'. Its domed Capitol is one of the finest buildings in the Southern States, where Governor George Wallace ruled for three terms, a period broken only by the term when his first wife served in that Office.

Mobile is the big port of Alabama, an old city with Civil War naval history, but today its centre is much restored with attractive artificial gas lamps lighting squares. The Mardi Gras staged here is second only to that of New Orleans. In the harbour the magnificent World War II battleship "Alabama" is open to the public, and alongside it is a submarine from the same era.

Towards the North of the State where the humidity is less sodden, there are some ultra-modern facets, with the big city of Birmingham full of steel plants and manufacturing industries. On top of a local mountain stands the second Statue of Liberty of America. A bit further North and one enters Huntsville, the home of Space Rockets where Dr Werner Von Braun had his headquarters during his post-war life with NASA. The Museum is open to visitors who can even enter some of the used spacecraft.

The Tennessee River, flowing towards the Mississippi from Chattanooga, crosses Alabama and enables Sheffield to be a major port. The dramatic locks at Sheffield are the deepest in the world, constructed on a scale only matched by the Panama Canal. A wild and dangerous river until the early 1930's, the Tennessee used to flood and destroy every year, but the Tennessee Valley Authority, set up during the Depression as one of the largest public works ever known, conquered it. The Mississippi itself, though, is still untamed although high levees help to control its spring flood.

Landscape

Rivers continue to play a vitally important part in the South's geography and economy, not just for the daily yield of catfish which are such a popular dish. One river not well known is the Red, in North Louisiana, on which the growing city of Shreveport stands. One day a TV series may be made based on the adventures of Captain Shreve who, almost alone, cleared this waterway of algae and plantlife to make it navigable back in the 1840's. It is the ninth longest river in the United States and still retains its distinctive red colour, especially in northern Louisiana.

Wherever one goes in true Deep South country there will be live oak trees, their branches dripping with silvery Spanish Moss. Never allow this stuff to touch bare skin; it is full of chiggers and other tiny insects. Hanging still in an atmosphere of oppressive heat, the live oak makes wonderful shade, but take care that it does not bite.

7.   The Great Plains

North Dakota, South Dakota, Nebraska, Kansas and Oklahoma

Background

Rivers play a vitally important part in the life and work of the United States even today. People talk about "friends on the Upper Connecticut Valley" or "He lives further up the Missouri". They tend not to indicate highways as a reference point, and certainly not railways (except for suburban lines in the East).

Two river valleys play a frontier role for this chapter. They are the Missouri and the Red River of the North. Going West across them leads on to the Great Plains, vast rolling empires of grassland which today feed the world with grain but 130 years ago were the stomping ground of enormous buffalo herds. One river does lead across the Plains through Nebraska to Colorado, where it divides into the North Platte and South Platte. Following its route proved very useful to the builders of the Union Pacific Railroad, which began in Omaha and reached the high plateau of Wyoming where the North Platte comes from, in two years.

Everybody knows the story of the buffalo, great heavy hairy animals called bison in America. Suffice it to say that when the big herds shared the Plains with Indians, there were reckoned to be 50 million of them, roughly divided into a north and south herd, all grass eaters enjoying the lush tall growth, migrating southwards in winter where the snow and cold were more moderate. The Plains Indians, equipped with horses which they inherited from the early Spanish explorers, lived off the buffalo, using every part of the animal for food, clothing, and lodging, but they only hunted a few hundred each season.

When the railways started across the Plains, particularly the new Union Pacific, they encountered buffalo in a dramatic way. In the late 1860's there are authentic accounts of trains being held up for six to eight hours while a herd crossed the tracks. Primitive, quickly laid metals (on which 25 miles an hour was a speedlimit for the West until 1895) broke under the weight of millions of hooves. There was widespread hunting, with passengers shooting from the open windows of trains and not able to gather the carcasses. People came from Europe, nobles from the Austro-Hungarian Empire included, just to shoot buffalo. The tongues of the dead animals became a sought-after delicacy.

But all this made little impression on the great herds. So the Union Pacific, and lesser railroads then under construction, employed hard-riding sharpshooters to kill the buffalo. Best known was William Cody (Buffalo Bill), whose personal 'score' is said to have exceeded 20,000.

The slaughter by the buffalo hunters was glamorised at the time and the

Buffalo Bill troop toured European capitals, even appearing before Queen Victoria on the stage in London. By 1877 the vast herds of heavy, surly beasts were gone, less than a thousand remaining in South Dakota and a few in the sanctuary of Yellowstone National Park (the first of its kind in the world, declared in 1872). With the buffalo perished also most of the Plains Indians. Settlers took over and soon the wide prairies were raising wheat and maize.

The Great Plains States, between the rivers and woodlands of Mid-America and the western mountains, are North Dakota, South Dakota, Nebraska, Kansas, and Oklahoma. Each one is bigger than England and Wales, ranging from 70,000 to 82,000 square miles. These prairies are indeed vast, seemingly limitless, rolling to the horizons, treeless and golden in late summer, frigid and white in winter. They all have an extreme climate, but enjoy early summer rains which help the crops (when these rains fail, as they do on infrequent occasions, everyone in the world feels it in the cost of bread).

The prairies are not a tourist attraction, nor can they be regarded as holiday zones, but there are pockets of interest. It is often said that they should be 'slept across', and both trans-continental trains and long distance buses arrange their main schedules so that they are crossed at night, or as much of them as can be traversed at speed in darkness. Flying over them merely means observing a sepia blur, or a white mist, from the windows.

In general, the prairies rise from East to West, and are rarely completely flat. Each State has mountains, many of them higher than Scotland's Ben Nevis. They all have lakes, nearly all the bigger ones man-made. Oklahoma, in fact, has more fresh water from its abundant lakes than any apart from Minnesota, where they are all natural.

North Dakota

The small town of Rugby, North Dakota, has an obelisk close to the railway station which marks the exact geographical centre of the North American continent, measured from the Panama Canal to Arctic Canada, and from East to West. North Dakota also has the Theodore Roosevelt National Memorial Park in the mountains on its western border, where summits up to 3,500 feet stand as buttes (isolated flat-topped rocky outcrops). On its border with Canada's Manitoba Province there is the beautiful International Peace Garden extending over more than 2000 acres. Driving this way into Canada a few years ago, I thought a British Passport might be rare at this crossing. "No", said the Immigration people, "we average 12 a day".

Bismark, on the upper Missouri River, is the capital of North Dakota, which with Mandan on the western side of the river boasts a population of about 60,000. It was founded in 1872 as Edwinton by the Northern Pacific Railway builders, but quickly had its name changed to attract German capital investment. It has the distinction of being the coldest capital in the United States during the bitter Prairie winters, with 50 below not unknown.

Built in 1933 Bismark's Capitol is a modern 18-storey structure, without traditional trappings. It is one of the 11 without a dome.

South Dakota

South Dakota has much more going for it as a tourist State, particularly

THE
GREAT
PLAINS

MINNESOTA

• Bottineau
• Minot
Grand
Forks

NORTH DAKOTA
Theodore Roosevelt
National Park
• Medora   • Bismarck

Fargo

Aberdeen

SOUTH DAKOTA
• Pierre
• Deadwood   *Black Hills*
National Forest
• Rapid City
Badlands National Park
Wind Cave National Park

Sioux Falls

NEBRASKA
Scottsbluff
South
Sioux City

IOWA

North Platte
Omaha

Grand Island
Lincoln

COLORADO

KANSAS
Topeka
Abilene •
Kansas City

MISSOURI

Dodge City
• Wichita

NEW MEXICO

OKLAHOMA
Tulsa
Oklahoma City

ARKANSAS

TEXAS
Anadarko
• Lawton

amid the Black Hills in the West. In these Hills, which are really mountains rising to Harney Peak, 7242 feet, one finds the historic Wild West town of Deadwood, noted for its Stage, (this ran to Cheyenne) and for the killing of Wild Bill Hickock in a saloon. Calamity Jane is buried in the local cemetery alongside him.

Custer made his last stand fighting the Sioux in 1876, the battleground being on the Little Bighorn which is over in Montana (a National Monument on Interstate 90 some 45 miles from Billings), but Custer township where his troops assembled is amid the Black Hills. Rapid City, population 45,000, is the jumping off point for exploring the Black Hills region; the city is on bus lines and has a moderately busy airport.

The number one attraction of the Black Hills is Mount Rushmore, 6,200 feet, on the eastern flank of which the faces of four presidents have been carved. The portraits of Washington, Jefferson, Lincoln, and Theodore Roosevelt are proportionate to full length figures 645 feet high, and were worked into the granite by the Swedish sculptor Gutzon Borglum with his son Lincoln and a small army of helpers on a Federal payroll. The concept began in 1927 and was completed 14 years later as one of the greatest memorials in the world, visited by two million people a year. Most coach or bus tours of the West stop here, and at Deadwood.

Inspired by the success of Mount Rushmore, a Polish sculptor decided that a similar tribute be paid to South Dakota's best known Indian chief, Crazy Horse. Korczak Ziolkowski actually worked on Mount Rushmore, but was a Boston sculptor previously. He came back to South Dakota in 1947, armed with a mere 174 Dollars

to start his project. The authorities gave him a mountain but he refused Federal help, later setting up the Crazy Horse Memorial Foundation. He married and had ten children, five sons eventually working on the mountain. Korczak died before seeing his vision completed, although he did blast and chip some ten million tons of granite from the Crazy Horse project. He died in 1987, aged 79.

In May 1981 I climbed with Korczak and one son to the top of the Indian's forming head, and later watched a blast clear 20,000 tons away from the horse. So gigantic is the statue that all four Mount Rushmore heads will fit into Crazy Horse's head!

On the ranges East of the Black Hills, South Dakota has a State-owned herd of buffalo 6,500 strong. These are the animals often seen on movies, careful camera work recapturing the days of the Great Plains. It is the biggest herd extant, though there are several thousands scattered in Yellowstone Park and elsewhere.

Capital of the State is tiny Pierre, on the Missouri River, hard to reach by public transport in the centre of the rectangular State and seldom on a tourist circuit. It does have an imposing capitol building with a capitol dome in copper, worked on by convicts when it was built in 1909. The locals call it 'Peer'.

Nebraska

Nebraska is a truly grain State, and on its huge capitol building at Lincoln (population 150,000) is the statue of a reaper on top of the dome, in keeping with the nickname 'Cornhusker State'. Omaha is the biggest city, having over half a million people. It is still headquarters of the Union Pacific Railroad, founded here in 1862. Famous Nebraskans include Fred

Astaire, Henry Fonda, and Harold Lloyd.

Kansas

Kansas is the archetypal prairie State, fertile plains sweeping mile upon mile but with a touch of the Old West at Dodge City and Cimarron. Capital is Topeka, with 125,000 population and a magnificent capitol building spreading over 16 acres. It has a dome of blue marble. Biggest city in Kansas is Wichita, about 300,000. Kansas City, while in Missouri, has an adjoining city across the river which is confusingly called Kansas City, Kansas. It is in this State where you can ride waggon trains, proper covered Conestogas going on five-day trail journeys. It is the prime international attraction bringing tourists to the State, with a true sense of adventure including camping out under the stars.

Oklahoma

Oklahoma, most southerly of the States of the Great Plains, is one of the most interesting areas of America for devotees of Indian history. The name means 'Home of the Red People', the place so many were taken to on foot after the 'Trail of Tears' from their Southeast hunting grounds. There are five tribes in Oklahoma today, all thriving despite their guaranteed homeland having been invaded in 1889 by a settlers' run. The borders were thrown open and tens of thousands of homesteaders rushed in at a fixed time, on horseback and on foot. A second 'run' was allowed in 1893, to the Cherokee Outlet.

The Indians of Oklahoma, known as the 'five civilised tribes', are Cherokees, Choctaw, Chickasaw, Creek, and Seminole (from Florida originally). They have done well, not only in agriculture but in oil and commerce, and many of the top

executives in those high rise Tulsa and Oklahoma offices are either pure or half-breed Indians. Will Rogers, the famous film star and aviator, was one of the latter.

First capital of Oklahoma after the white men broke in, was established at Guthrie, a red brick town with a lot of character. Then it was moved about 30 miles South to Oklahoma City, now the centre of State government. The capitol building is famous for having working oil wells in the grounds. It is a wide Palladian building without a dome, although there was talk of constructing a dome to mark the centenary of the 1889 'run'. This has not materialised, but they still talk of building one for the hundredth anniversary of the '93', regarded as the more important settlers push westwards.

Western Oklahoma is ranch country, clearly part of the true 'West', and its rodeos are part and parcel of life and entertainment throughout the State. There is a National Cowboy Hall of Fame in Oklahoma City, with a special John Wayne memorial section. Ultra-modern high-rise in its downtown area, this capital is one of the dullest in America, everything, including public transport, shutting down at 7 pm, although there is much activity in outlying Malls. Mainly 'dry', the city is strongly Baptist and called "the buckle of the Bible belt".

A more vigorous city is Tulsa, 150 miles Northeast on the Arkansas River, where attractions include a splendid opera house, the Thomas Gilcrease Institute of Art and History, and some fine shopping streets. Some of the hotels are excellent and so is the architecture of oil-related buildings. The Oral Roberts University has an amazing pair of hands in prayer rising several hundred feet. The city, with half a million population, is even a port, big ships getting up the Arkansas via a lock system.

To the East, Oklahoma rises in the Ozark Mountains, a range across the borders into corners of Arkansas, Missouri, and Kansas. Less remote than in the days of the 'Hillbillies', the Ozarks are still quiet and rural, with pleasant lakes and small resorts. In their foothills are some Indian villages, some of which have craft demonstrations and even restaurants featuring traditional Indian dishes.

Although the Ozark summits reach 2880 feet, the high point of Oklahoma is far to the West in the Cimarron strip, where Black Mesa rises to 4973 feet.

Horses feature strongly in Oklahoma life with genuine cowboys using them, not only for rodeos, and numerous horse farms breed Morgan horses. They say there are half as many horses as humans in the State, and the population is close to three million people.

8. Mountain West

Colorado, Eastern Utah, Wyoming, Montana
Colorado/Rocky Mountains

When explorers pushed westwards over the Great Plains and came across a great range of mountains rising sheer in jagged granite masses to formidable heights, they called them the 'Shining Mountains'. Nowhere was this title more apt than in Colorado, where the glinting escarpments soared up to eternal snows. They presented a barrier, a wall, hindering any onward progress to the West until high passes had been found and conquered.

The Spanish explorers of an earlier era had come into Colorado from the South, looking for gold and silver (which they found), and they named the region on account of the red colour of the fast-flowing river thundering down from the mountains to the West and South. It was mostly in Colorado territory that they lost so many horses, animals which enjoyed the lush grazing on their own until Indian tribes captured them.

The term 'Rocky Mountains' came into general use soon after the Louisiana Purchase attached the area to the United States. In 1806 Lieutenant Zebulon Pike explored the range in detail, nearly scaling a major summit which bears his name today. He was not quite correct in believing Pike's Peak, at 14,110 feet, was the highest, but there is little difference among them, no less than 54 of the Colorado Rockies exceeding 14,000 feet with the actual supreme summit being Elbert, at 14,333 feet. But Pike's Peak is easier to climb and less than 85 years after the Lieutenant had just failed to reach the top, a steam cog railway was pushing tourists up from Manitou Springs. This is now a diesel rack and pinion line belonging to a Swiss company. The line has a flawless safety record over its century of frequent journeying to the highest point reached by rail in North America.

There is still no finer or more dramatic way of appreciating the great wall of Rocky Mountains than by taking the trans-continental train "California Zephyr" from Denver to Salt Lake City, or making the shorter journey to Glenwood Springs. As soon as mile-high Denver is left the train faces a gigantic wall of mountains which it tackles full face on a tremendous gradient, eased somewhat by the five miles long Moffat Tunnel (opened in 1929). AMTRAK runs just the one train over this Denver and Rio Grande main line, doing the scenic run in daylight with double-decked Superliner cars and a sightseer lounge enabling passengers to enjoy the spectacle. The highway out of Denver is wide but less scenic and crosses by way of the Eisenhower Tunnel, opened in the 1960's.

Before the Moffat Tunnel was built, the main line used to go South to Pueblo on the high plains of eastern

71

Colorado and then strike westwards along the Arkansas River, passing through America's second largest canyon, the Royal Gorge of the Arkansas. So deep and steep is this canyon that the track was suspended from the rock by cantilevers. It is still there but used only by occasional freights or a Sunday excursion from Denver.

Trains used to stop as the excursion does, and by means of a type of mechanical 'toboggan' slanting up the rock, passengers were taken to the lip of the gorge for the views. The 'toboggan' is in use today for road travellers, who cross the Royal Gorge suspension bridge, highest in America, for a complete tour, including a 'shoot-out' in a mock Western town on the canyon rim, where stage coach rides are on offer.

Many of Colorado's romantic old narrow gauge railroad lines into the mountains have been restored, among them Cripple Creek, and the incredible Georgetown Loop. Further West the Durango and Silverton, 40 miles long and climbing into the San Juan mountains to 9000 feet, is the most successful narrow gauge line in the Western Hemisphere, while the Antonito-based Cumbres and Toltec, climbing over the 10,000 foot Toltec Pass into New Mexico, is the longest, a full day's ride of scenic grandeur. The State's Railroad Museum is at Golden, some 10 miles from Denver, where another small line, starting from Heritage Square, makes a short trip winding through the foothills of the main wall of the Rockies. This is the High Country Railroad, only 24 inches gauge. All these are steam operated.

Close to Golden those interested may find a visit to the Coors brewery worthwhile. This low alcohol beer used to be confined to Colorado, but its reputation as a clean and wholesome brew made from water cascading down from the summits of the Rockies led to it being on sale in most parts of America, with special emphasis on the states which are near-dry. A cold Coors on a hot day is just about the most refreshing drink available, and with a mere 15 percent reduction in alcohol content could even be sold to Saudi Arabia!

The State of Colorado is a perfect rectangle, the eastern third high plain, the central and western two-thirds very high mountains interspersed with valleys, no land being below 6000 feet. Although nearly twice the size of Austria and Hungary combined, Colorado ranks only eighth in the Union. A popular local quip to Texans who boast of the vastness of their State is: "If Colorado was to be rolled flat it would be the biggest State in America." It is already, in majesty and spectacle.

The first settlers arrived in what was to become Denver in 1858, to set up stores and lodging houses for miners working in the high mountains not many miles away. By 1876 there was enough population to declare Denver the capital of the new State of Colorado. The beautiful capitol building, with its narrow golden dome, is exactly one mile above sea level, measured at its corner stone. In and around the city the air is the cleanest and purest of any big American urban complex, and although there are extremes of temperature it is always exhilarating with 'champagne quality' as some visitors claim. Even the Denver buses help the atmosphere; most of them are electric-driven by massive batteries, while solar power motivates some of them.

Down in the Mesa Verde country in the South West, four borders meet,

Glacier National Park

Glasgow •

NORTH DAKOTA

Missoula

Great Falls

Drummond •

Helena

Butte •

MONTANA

West
Yellowstone

Billings

SOUTH DAKOTA

Yellowstone
National Park

Bighorn
National
Forest

Sheridan

Shoshone
National Forest

IDAHO

Grand Teton
National Park

Jackson

WYOMING

• Casper

• Laramie

Cheyenne •

NEBRASKA

Salt Lake City

Park City

Provo •

Arches National
Monument

UTAH

Canyonlands
National Park

Steamboat Springs

Rocky Mountain
National Park

• Estes Park

• Denver

Vail •

NEVADA

Aspen •

Colorado Springs

KANSAS

Zion
National Park

Bryce Canyon
National Park

Royal Gorge •

COLORADO

ARIZONA

Mesa Verde National Park

MOUNTAIN WEST

NEW MEXICO

the only place in the United States where this happens. Utah, New Mexico, Arizona and Colorado touch at 'Four Corners'. There are so many magnificent parts of Colorado it is only possible to pick out a few highlights, but a rental car is needed to get around the West and South West if the best is to be enjoyed. I have driven over what is called the 'Million Dollar Highway' from Silverton to Montrose over the high Uncompahgre Plateau, dominated by the 14,306 foot peak of the same name. There are places along the twisting road – sometimes with a vertical wall of rock on one side and a drop of 3000 feet on the other – which reflect the feelings of early pioneers driving mule wagons over the then dirt trail. One is Telluride (converted from 'to Hell you ride'), and, once the gradient lessens and the road seems safer, there comes Ouray, reckoned to be named after an Indian chief but most drivers think it stems from 'Hooray'.

My favourite place in Colorado, perhaps in all the United States, for its sheer spectacle and the feeling of awe it induces, is the Black Canyon of the Gunnison. It is a National Monument with Rangers controlling the entry road, but after that the visitor is on his own, in a dramatic wilderness leading up to Monarch Pass through the remote Sawatch Mountains.

Colorado has some of the best skiing in the world, with high country powdered snow which attracts international winter sports enthusiasts. During the 1989–90 winter, more than 10,000 Britons alone journeyed to the Rockies to enjoy holidays which the Alps could not equal. Vail and Aspen are the two most fashionable and costly resorts, quite recently developed and expanded, with top quality ski facilities, but there are many more coming along, like Breckenridge in the region of Tennessee Pass whose 10,424 feet altitude was reached by the pre-1929 main rail line of the Rio Grande Railroad on its way to Grand Junction.

Eastern Utah

Crossing into Utah, the mountains fall away into high desert country through which the Colorado River carves a winding path, frequently boiling into white water stretches over rapids. Both rail and highway pass through the small town of Thompson, and some 30 miles to the South of it lies the incredible Arches National Park. The hot little town of Moab is the centre for visits to this amazing place, where natural stone arches abound in the 73,000 acres of canyons and shapes.

Arches National Park is the pride of eastern Utah, yet its very existence was unknown until 1926 when surveyors for the Rio Grande Railroad happened upon it. So far, 90 arches have been discovered, the best known being Delicate Arch, slim and tapered and nearly 100 feet high, also Landscape Arch, the longest known natural stone bridge.

To the South are the Canyonlands, inaccessible apart from using four-wheel drive vehicles on rocky tracks. It is a wilderness of stone shapes and desert, with no accommodation but plenty of visitors, who must camp or lie out under the stars in sleeping bags. The Green River from the North flows into the Colorado at a junction which can only be viewed from 2000 foot bluffs or from the rivers themselves (and intrepid tourists ride inflatables under skilled pilotage through this confluence where white water rises in overfalls to a dozen feet or more).

East and Southeast Utah has some wild country indeed, much easier to reach since 1976 when as a bi-centennial commemoration the few roads were paved or at least shingled. There are giant 'lost world' mesas which remain unclimbed, and some areas are still marked on maps as 'not yet surveyed'. Beyond the Dirty Devil River lies Capitol Reef National Park where giant monoliths rear from the arid valley floors. There are pre-historic Indians paintings. Legend has it that Butch Cassidy hid out in this stone wilderness.

Torrey Canyon, from which a giant supertanker which crashed onto the Isles of Scilly in 1967 took its name, is at the northern entrance. Torrey calls itself a city, and it does boast two motels, a general store, and a filling station – the latter welcomed because it is 141 miles to the next one, at Hanksville. In all the mainland USA no greater feeling of remoteness, yet peace and freedom, is experienced than in Southeast Utah. This big State, of 85,000 square miles, nearly twice the size of Greece, has a population of less than 1½ millions, and some 40 percent of those live in Salt Lake City.

Both road and rail, heading Northwest through Utah to the more fertile regions of Provo and Salt Lake City, must labour up to Soldier Summit, 7477 feet. The town of Helper, at the start of the climb gets its name from the Helper (Banking) Engines, sometimes five of them, to overcome the gradient. They are based here; all diesels now, with a smaller workforce.

Brigham Young led his Mormons on the long trek away from their tormentors in the eastern States and reached the shore of the Great Salt Lake in 1847. There he established the

city, enjoying complete autonomy and Church of the Latter Day Saints practices for 30 years. But 19 years after his death in 1877, the growing populations in neighbouring states and desires for a link-up among the Mormons, led to Utah becoming the 45th State of the Union in 1896. While Mormons continue their strict codes of religion and conduct, they eased regulations for visitors by 1946. Before that, coffee could not even be purchased in cafes. The State is still officially dry but liquor may be obtained and consumed privately. Mormons have lost some of their power in State government.

Southern Utah has its scenic wonders as well as the other areas, notably Bryce Canyon, Zion National Park, and Cedar Breaks National Monument. The highest peak in Utah, though, lies far to the East of Salt Lake City, in the High Uintas Primitive Area, where King's Peak rears up to 13,528 feet. There are no roads, nor even trails, leading anywhere near it. Backpacker climbers do occasionally make the ascent.

Wyoming

Another perfectly rectangular State to the North of Utah and Colorado is spacious Wyoming, land of cattle and horses, mighty mountains and fast rivers, but very few people. In all its 97,000 square miles it has just over 400,000 inhabitants, about four in every square mile (Belgium has 835). This is truly a country of wide open spaces; from its high plains always a distant glimpse of snowclad mountains.

The Overland Trail took a route across Wyoming's 7000 foot grassy plains tucked in a wide break of the Rockies. They rolled their wagons through what are now the cities of

Cheyenne and Laramie with relative ease, their trials and tribulations to come later with the desert and the Sierra Nevadas. Cheyenne became capital in 1890 and is still by far the largest city in the State with about 42,000 people. Laramie, 50 miles West, is second city, with 23,000, set at 7000 feet above sea level.

This became the line of the Union Pacific Railroad, crossing the high plain at Sherman Hill between Cheyenne and Laramie, before descending gently through the hills of South Wyoming on its way to Green River and, eventually, Ogden in Utah. Today's Inter-State Highway 80 follows virtually the same route.

Wyoming's crowning glory is the magnificent range of mountains known as the Grand Tetons, in the Northwest of the State beyond the Snake River and Jackson Lake. Their jagged, spectacular peaks reach a climax at Grand Teton, 13,766 feet, and even the pass through them which the highway from Jackson Hole traverses on its way westwards is at eight and a half thousand.

Because of its beauty and the ski facilities in winter plus high altitude 'Dude' ranches in summer, Jackson Hole has become an important tourist area. Horse riding, fishing, raft trips on the fierce Snake River (not as tough as the Salmon in Idaho nor the Colorado), the many ranches taking paying guests, and the access to the South entrance of Yellowstone National Park, contribute to the region's popularity. It is a long way from the nearest rail station for those without a car (highly desirable here unless on a bus tour) but Jackson Springs Stage Line offers a fairly good scheduled bus service to Rock Springs.

Wyoming is the home of the Shoshone Tribe, spread over large reservations amid the Shoshone National Forest and a little-known mountain range called Bridger-Teton, an off-shoot of the main Rockies. They keep very much to themselves and do not welcome casual visitors, although one unusual guest they had when I was in their territory once was a Shoshone-speaking Japanese! Their mountains contain vast herds of elk, which come down into lower regions during the severe winter. They are fed by Federal funds at that time, and visitors may go in horse-drawn carts to see this strange spectacle.

The town of Cody on the eastern edge of Shoshone lands has the Buffalo Bill Museum, winner of International awards. It is in fact the Buffalo Bill Historic Center, containing excellent examples of Western art, and a Plains Indian Museum. The town, founded by William Cody in 1897, has a population of about 5000.

Most of the world's first National Park, Yellowstone, created in 1872 to preserve wilderness and wild life, lies within Wyoming, but a tiny strip is shared with Montana, the State to the North. The South entrance is about 24 miles North of Jackson Hole, busy, and Ranger controlled in summer, but in winter very different. I went in there one February in a snowcoach, the temperature slowly edging up from a morning low of 32 below, and we crossed the gateway lying 22 feet below us in hard-packed wind-driven snow!

Yellowstone is vast, bigger even than Alaska's Denali and in acres it exceeds 2¼ million. The Grand Loop road, which most motoring visitors take, is 142 miles long. But the highlight is Old Faithful, a hot geyser which erupts hourly, sending its spume to a height of at least 150 feet. Not far away is the giant wooden lodge where many people seek to stay, although there are other motels and lodges scattered around the Park. Old Faithful is the most reliable geyser, but there are dozens more (at least 200) with the Norris Geyser Basin yielding some of the best spectacles.

Off the main roads one can often see grizzly bears, and always buffalo and elk. The 'Grand Canyon of the Yellowstone' is favoured by many not only for its scenery (there is a waterfall twice the height of Niagara) but for its wildlife on the rims. July and August are crowded times these days, with traffic jams forming. At such heights winter comes early and September nights are always below freezing, but this is a better time for peace and quiet.

Yellowstone's northern boundaries are in the State of Montana, where the Gardiner Gate and the Silver Gate are located. In fact, Park Headquarters are on the border, at Mammoth Hot Springs. Eastern Idaho also has a thin fringe of the Yellowstone but there are no gates, the nearest being West Yellowstone in Montana. The famous Continental Divide runs close to here, on its thousand mile, twisting route. It marks the point where rivers flow either to the Atlantic (eventually) or the Pacific.

Montana

Montana is a very large State, 147,000 square miles of it divided between high grassy plains and mountains. Only three-quarters of a million people live here in a region almost as big as the Kingdom of Spain. The capital is Helena, declared in 1889, whose capitol building dome reflects the major product of Montana – copper. Vast quantities of the mineral are

mined amid the Montana Rockies, with the city of Butte (pronounced Bute) the 'copper capital', and the mine at Anaconda overshadowed by the giant peaks Mount Haggin and Mount Evans (both above 10,500 feet) the biggest in the State. Incidentally, the deepest and widest copper mine in the world is in Utah, a tourist attraction some 20 miles southwest of Salt Lake City.

They call Montana the 'Big Sky Country' as anyone who travels through it on a clear day soon appreciates. The crisp air and altitude (even the plains are around 4000 feet and the very lowest point in the State, on the Kootenay River, is 1800 feet) create amazing visibility.

There is a prairie town in the extreme Northwest on the edge of the Blackfeet Indian Reservation called Browning. Road and rail pass through it to tackle the main wall of the northern Rockies at Marais Pass, only a dozen miles away. It is a dramatic transition from the summer brown of the high plains to the white and deep green fastnesses of the mountains. The Great Northern Railway, part of Burlington Northern, carries AMTRAK's "Empire Builder" on this line. Another main line threads the State to the South, the Northern Pacific Railway, but no passenger service runs where once the "North Coast Limited" and "Mainstreeter" used to cross the Continent. Northern Pacific, also part of Burlington Northern, climbs through the Rockies at Homestake Pass, 6375 feet, but Marais to the North is the lowest Rockies crossing, at 5216 feet.

Once at the Pass, however, both road and rail are into a wonderland of mountains and glaciers, rushing rivers, waterfalls, and thick forests. This is Glacier National Park, a great spread of spectacular territory merged across the Canadian Border with the Waterton Lakes National Park. The lower country between Browning and the mountain wall stretches to the famous 49th parallel and into Canada as the International Peace Park.

Glacier Park is only open in its entirety from June to early October, but snow may stop road traffic at any time and often closes it for the winter by mid-September. Trains run all year, snowploughs keeping the line clear but the stations giving entry to the Park are not open between October and May. There are some 50 glaciers of varying sizes in the park, the largest being Grinnell, which has compacted blue ice 400 feet thick.

Montana does not end even when the high mountains do, for there is great country beyond. Two towns, Whitefish and Kalispell, are tourist points for exploring the Flathead country including the huge, natural, Flathead Lake, but caution and courtesy should be exercised if crossing the wide open spaces of the Flathead Indian Reservation.

In high summer, a road can be used going from Whitefish around the edge of the Flathead National Forest and into West Glacier. It then twists and turns and climbs through the heart of the Glacier National Park past Lake MacDonald, over the 6664 foot Logan Pass and out at the hamlet of St Mary 19 miles from Canada. They call it "Going to the Sun" Highway, reckoned to be the most spectacular road in the world. Having picnicked along it, I find no reason to dispute the claim.

Miami (Florida)
Beach and Intra-Coastal Canal

Tulsa (Oklahoma)
'Hands at Prayer' monument

New Orleans (Lousiana)
The French Quarter

S.E. Utah
Arches National Park

San Antonio (Texas) - The Alamo

California
Yosemite National Park

Oahu Island, (Hawaii)
Off Waikiki Beach

Yukon (Alaska)
White Pass in winter

9. The Great Southwest

Texas, New Mexico, Arizona, Southern California

Sunbelt

The sun beams down on the huge southern arc of the United States from Texas to California, a two thousand mile stretch of country rightly regarded as the 'Sun Belt'. Sunsets are famous for their dramatic colours and are equally welcome as a lessening of heat. It is not surprising that the name "Sunset Limited" has been bestowed for many decades upon the crack train running from Houston in Texas to Los Angeles, California. Each of the two evenings of its travel, passengers have a view of the sun going down in flaming glory, dipping into mountains or desert.

Texas, New Mexico, Arizona, and Southern California are the four states making up the 'Golden Southwest', regions closely associated with the history of wars with neighbouring Mexico, of Apache Indian battles, stage coaches dusting through remote landscapes, shoot-ups in cow-towns, and massive cattle herds seeking sparse pastures.

Rather suprisingly to those who do not know this Southwest 'Empire' there are other associations, other things to see. Such as the biggest rice paddies outside Burma, a higher and more rugged wall of Rocky Mountains than even Montana throws up against routes to the West, and a lake so far below sea level it is only a few feet above the Dead Sea of the Middle East.

Texas

Texas is the largest State among the contiguous '48', so big that it could swallow Morocco (which to some extent it resembles) and still leave room for Portugal. From 1836 to 1845 Texas was an independent Republic, which it has never forgotten, and became the 'Lone Star State' only when financial considerations (among which was the costs of its embassies in Europe) forced it to join the Union. Joining the Confederates 15 years later it tried to break with Washington but lost.

The vast region was just a wasteland with long-horned cattle running wild when Spain in 1811 simply gave it away to anyone who would come and colonise it. The British and Germans did so, in almost equal numbers, joined by new Americans from the recently independent East. Mexico, soon independent from Spain, thought Texas must belong to them as it had been Spanish and that is why the 1836 battles were fought, Texans losing at the Alamo in San Antonio but winning at San Jacinto near Houston. Look at the Alamo Memorial, preserved as it was when it fell, and see where the dead came from – many parts of England and Germany as well as newly formed American states.

Once huge ranches were established, and one of them, the King Ranch in the extreme South, is the biggest in America with a total acreage exceeding that of the State of

Delaware, the cattle had to be moved to railheads for northern and eastern markets. The arduous, months long, trek followed the famous Chisholm Trail to Dodge City, Kansas.

Oil transformed the Texas economy early in the 20th Century and made many fortunes, helping to build up the plains city of Dallas. Although in some decline these days, oil remains important, but petro-chemicals and manufacturing have overtaken it. The city of Dallas has become world-famous due to the television series, bringing countless thousands of tourists to see 'South Fork Ranch' which is real (and open to visitors at a price) some 20 miles on the outskirts. High rise Dallas, the eighth largest in the nation but fourth in wealth, sits astride the Trinity River in North Texas. John Neely Bryan, a Tennessee frontiersman, founded the place in 1844 and named it "after my friend Dallas" (actually US Vice-President George Miffin Dallas).

The banking, insurance, and oil centre of the Southwest, Dallas has overtaken its big neighbour Fort Worth 30 miles to the West, where some of the largest stockyards in the world are located. The two metro-complexes have grown towards each other (but in between is Arlington where the massive theme park 'Six Flags Over Texas' attracts millions of people every year – the six flags being Spain, Mexico, France, Lone Star Republic, Confederacy, and the Stars and Stripes). Also in between Dallas and Fort Worth is the world's largest airport, the first with an intensive free automated train system, some rides between terminals taking up to twenty minutes.

Texas has been noted for its claims to being the biggest and having the largest of anything. Foreigners and Americans alike tend to poke fun at Texans for this trait, less so since 1959 when Alaska was admitted to the Union, reducing Texas to second position. The Governor of Alaska reportedly said that if Texans didn't like it he would divide Alaska into two and that would put Texas in *third place*!

From a tourist point of view, much of Texas is boring with limitless vistas of open country, often flat. It is hot and dry in summer, cold and fairly dry in winter, the rainy season mostly in early summer. Regions of greater scenic interest lie in the South and Southwest. With a long coastline on the Gulf of Mexico there is a big area from Corpus Christi down to the border with Mexico which is called 'The Texas Tropical Coast'. Padre Island, 150 miles long and mostly unspoiled, is an offshore sand-spit with hotels and resorts at its northern end.

One must have a car to reach and travel on Padre Island, with access limited to two bridges 140 miles apart and one free ferry at the top end across Aransas Pass. There is plenty of warm winter sunshine and glorious beaches, while the bird life is unparalleled for Texas. The southerly bridge leads to Port Isabel, Brownsville on the Mexican border, and Harlingen, base for the amazing Confederate Air Force with its prize collection of vintage aircraft. The "Colonels" of the C.A.F. go to air shows all over the United States, re-enacting 'Tora Tora Tora' (the bombing of Pearl Harbor) and the Battle of Britain (with their real Spitfires and Heinkels).

Texas on the Gulf extends round in an arc with a series of off-shore sandy islands to the major port of Galveston. The island it stands on is a popular resort and daytripper spot for

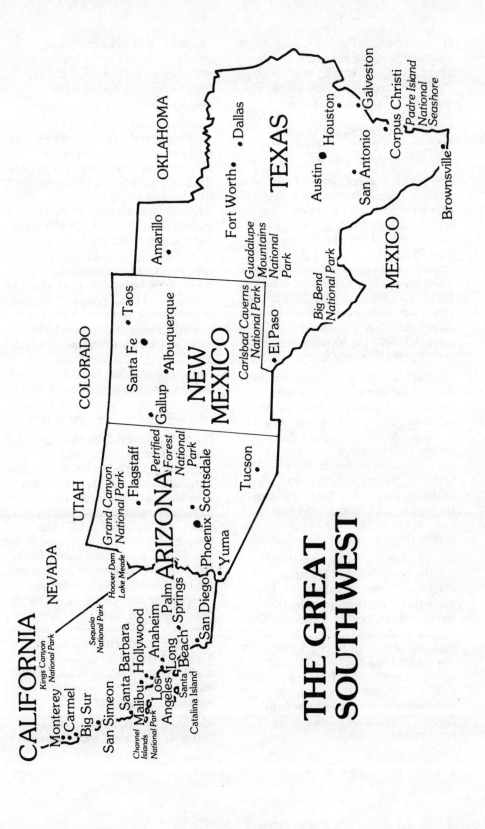

THE GREAT
SOUTH WEST

CALIFORNIA

NEVADA

UTAH

COLORADO

ARIZONA

NEW
MEXICO

TEXAS

OKLAHOMA

MEXICO

Monterey
Carmel
Big Sur
San Simeon
Santa Barbara
Malibu
Hollywood
Los
Angeles
Anaheim
Long
Beach
Santa
Catalina Island
San Diego
Palm
Springs
Yuma
Phoenix
Scottsdale
Tucson
Flagstaff
Gallup
Santa Fe
Taos
Albuquerque
El Paso
Amarillo
Fort Worth
Dallas
Austin
San Antonio
Houston
Galveston
Corpus Christi
Brownsville

Kings Canyon
National Park
Sequoia
National Park
Hoover Dam
Lake Mead
Grand Canyon
National Park
Petrified
Forest
National
Park
Channel
Islands
National Park
Carlsbad Caverns
National Park
Guadalupe
Mountains
National
Park
Big Bend
National Park
Padre Island
National
Seashore

Houston people. The giant conglomeration of Houston, 50 miles up a canal, (and on this canal watch out for the preserved First World War battleship "Texas", also the San Jacinto Battle Memorial towering 570 feet). To the East of the Canal is NASA's Space City, where Control speaks to the Astronauts.

Few people find hot, humid Houston a pleasant city but it does have plenty of interest in and around it. Some 2½ million live here in an immense 541 square miles of city and suburb less than 50 feet above sea level. Sometimes in winter a 'Norther' blows down from colder States and can knock the temperature down from 66 degrees to 26 degrees Fahrenheit in three hours. But in summer few breezes relieve the 95 degrees heat and 85 percent humidity.

The flat lands are marshy to East and West of the city and this is where Texas rice is grown in profusion, the well-liked American long-grain rice. In those paddy fields there are also crayfish, which thrive on the rice while the rice itself is helped by their presence, the result being two valuable crops. Giant prawns (called shrimps in USA) come from deeper Gulf waters and are landed all over the northern shore, selling at modest cost.

It is a ride of 165 miles through dull country going West of Houston to reach the Texas capital, Austin. I have made that trip many times, by train plane, and car, but have seen nothing but low prairie and cattle. It is much the same driving or taking a train or plane from Houston to Dallas (240 miles). There is talk which has been going on for years about making an ultra-high speed railway triangle to connect these cities quickly and comfortably.

However, Austin looms like an oasis and rewards its visitors handsomely with a magnificent capitol building below a shining marble dome second only to Washington's.

Austin, named after Stephen Fuller Austin the early Texan coloniser who died just after the defeat of the Mexicans, was selected as Capital of the State in 1845, after Houston lost that honour at the end of the Republic. It is a small city by Texan standards, with about 125,000 people, but it is pleasantly sited on a Colorado River (not the big one) amid gentle hills. Artificial Lake Austin is surrounded by good houses which are low cost even these days. Congress Avenue leads up to the dominating capitol building and is lined by admirable shops selling goods which are cheap by East standards. The University of Texas is in the heart of the city, sprouting a tall tower which was once the venue of a mad sniper who killed more than twenty people.

Going Southwest from the capital for 80 miles brings you to one of America's most remarkable big cities, San Antonio. It is a sprawl of more than two million people, with big military camps on the outskirts, and in years gone by it was a dull place suffering fierce heat. They used to say that "The Devil himself uses a fan in San Antone". But urban renewal and the creation of a lovely waterway through the city, called 'Paseo del Rio', has changed all that. There are boat trips with musicians, fine restaurants lining the banks, and cool plazas. The big local brewery, Lone Star, quenches the thrist of thousands who sit in beer gardens overlooking the waters.

Major attraction, shrine might be a better word, is the Alamo, standing in ruins in the heart of Downtown. This Mission, put up by the Spanish in 1718, was where 187 defenders died holding off 5000 Mexicans led by General Santa Anna. One woman escaped, to tell General Sam Houston of the disaster, enabling him to muster sufficient forces to beat Santa Anna a few months later at San Jacinto. But San Antonio is half Mexican today, the city bilingual, the food largely 'Tex-Mex', although there are excellent German restaurants and the usual fast-food American ones.

It was in 1968 that San Antonio blossomed into a tourist city, when they staged the Hemi-Sphere, a sort of local 'World's Fair'. Its symbol, the Tower of the Americas, rising to 622 feet, is found above Hemi-Sphere Plaza, and it is well worth going to the observation deck for distant views to the Texas Hill Country and for the lay-out of the city. Like the cities of the Pacific North West, San Antonio has a good transportation system which is free by bus around El Centro, a 25 square block Downtown. Do visit the Spanish Governor's Palace on Military Plaza, the only complete colonial mansion in the State, built in 1749.

The Texas Hill Country is some 40 miles Northwest of the city, with Bandera at the heart of it. Here one finds several Dude ranches, popular with British and German holidaymakers. To the South, after about 150 miles of mundane travel along Highway 35, the city of Laredo is reached, the American border town on the famous Rio Grande. Across the bridge lies the Mexican city of Nuevo Laredo, terminus of the Mexican railway system. A former railway bridge, now in poor condition, also crossed the Rio Grande and once carried through trains all the way from Chicago to Mexico City. Considerable numbers of European travellers cross this border.

Striking due West on Highway 90 from San Antonio or on the tracks of the Southern Pacific Railroad carrying the AMTRAK superliner train "Sunset Limited" it is about 165 miles to the next town of size, Del Rio, on the Mexican border opposite Ciudad Acuna. Driving this hot and not very scenic road, I passed through the hamlet of Bracketville and saw an incredible sight in the arid land to the North. I turned off towards it, to find a large full size movie set, with everything from a replica of the Alamo to a Wild West street. There was a caretaker in his office who showed me round, pointing out that many films had been made here on this permanent set with authentic dry hills in the background, and cheaper – much cheaper – Texas prices for the Hollywood financiers to consider.

Road and rail plod on to the Northwest after Del Rio, crossing the Pecos River after about 40 miles. This once marked the limit of what passed for law and order in the Old West. Some 20 miles beyond the high road and rail bridges over this historic river the tiny hamlet of Langtry is encountered. This was the long-term home of Judge Roy Bean, the man who declared himself the 'Law Beyond the Pecos' but whose main claim to fame was his love of Lily Langtry. He worked at the Southern Pacific Construction Camp then called Vinegaroon and was a devoted fan of the opera singer (mistress of King Edward VII), even renaming his hamlet after her and exchanging warm letters with the Jersey Lily! Eventually, after much persuasion, she decided to visit him during an opera tour of America, but when her private railway coach was detached from the "Sunset

Limited" at Langtry in 1907, she was greeted with the news that Judge Bean had died of a heart attack only three days earlier. In that heat she was too late even for the funeral.

Another 50 miles westwards brings road and rail to the foothills of the Rockies, while over to the left loom the giants of the Big Bend National Park, where the Rio Grande makes a huge loop around the Chisos Mountains (highest is Mount Emory, 7835 feet) and roars through Santa Elena Canyon. This is dangerous country to get lost in, but staying on the marked road and trails is safe enough; the Park is full of mountain lions, rattlesnakes, and tarantulas, plus fierce summer heat.

Highway 90 follows the Southern Pacific tracks into the Texas Rockies, while further North, Highway 10 crosses ranch country via Kerrville (limit of the Dude Ranch Hill Country), Junction, Sonora and Fort Stockton. Much further North, Highway 20 links the Dallas–Fort Worth Metro-Zone with Abilene and the Odessa–Midland complex, with 350 mostly featureless miles. All three routes eventually come together at Van Horn, 4000 feet up in the Sierra Diablo Mountains. The highest peaks in Texas, "El Capitan" and "Guadalupe" (8–9,000ft) are 60 miles north of Van Horn.

Various named mountain ranges make up the Texas Rockies, such as the Glass Mountains, the Christmas Range, the Chinatis, the Apache Mountains, the Delawares, the Quitman Mountains, the Finlays, and the Sierra Velas, to name just some of them. Over in Mexico they are all the Sierra Madres. These mountains are all part of the immensely long Rocky system which forms the backbone of North America from the Yukon to Panama.

Road and rail on the more interesting route to the West go through Marathon and up to Alpine, a high point where Sol Ross State University is located. The summit of the railroad is at Paisano on the Del Norte Pass, 5074 feet, with the nearby highway a few feet higher. Both descend gently after that to El Paso, the major city of West Texas, on the border with New Mexico and on the northern bank of the Rio Grande. To show how big Texas is, the distance from Alpine to El Paso is 220 miles, and that is only a quarter of the way across the State. From South to North, say from Brownsville to Amarillo, it is 784 miles, and there is still 100 miles to go to the northern border into Oklahoma's Panhandle.

El Paso, full name El Paso del Norte, is sprawled across the Pass between the American Rockies and the Mexican Sierra Madres where the Franklin Mountains are cut through by the Rio Grande, a route used by road and rail. The city is 3760 feet above sea level, famed for its intense sunshine and dry atmosphere, with only about 15 days a year when the sun does not shine. It is considered a great place for sufferers from arthritis and rheumatism.

Across the Rio Grande bridges lies Ciudad Juarez, one of Mexico's largest cities. Residents of both cities may come and go freely; two things which bring Mexicans to the American city are cheap photocopying and faxing facilities, while Americans go over the border for cheap dental treatment! Tourists criss-cross for all kinds of general purposes, many of them to go to Chihuahua for the relatively new and very scenic Chihuahua Pacifico trans-Mexico Railway through Copper Canyon to Los Mochis on the Pacific. This journey is 580 miles; to Mexico City it is a formidable 1300 miles.

El Paso is a splendid place for a break on any southern trans-continental journey. Take the cable car up from the city to the summit of Mount Franklin, the very first peak of the American Rockies, actually within city limits! The Tigua Indian Reservation is close to town, a 'pueblo', meaning settled people, who grow crops and have a culture based on home life rather than hunting. Some 35 miles out of town is Indian Cliffs Ranch, noted for its trail rides, covered wagons and barbeques – voted one of the top ten tourist attractions by German visitors to the United States. The whole region is story-packed from Wild West days, from shoot-outs to Mexican raids, and was an important stop on the Butterfield Stage route.

New Mexico

A few miles out of El Paso heading North West, road, rail and river pass into New Mexico. All along the Rio Grande there are high barbed wire fences against wet-backs, the name given to illegal Mexican immigrants who wade and swim the river to try and enter the United States for relatively highly-paid, no-questions-asked menial jobs. But in New Mexico the costly fencing has fallen away, and any train passenger can see by day from the high-level scenic coaches scores of Mexicans attempting the river crossing. From Highway 25, which leads to Albuquerque and eventually to Santa Fe, the capital, intruders cannot easily be seen – it is set well over to the East of the rail tracks.

New Mexico is an almost perfect square, except for a bit jutting into Mexico which encompasses Animas and Big Hatchet Peaks in the extreme Southwest. It is high and dry, and more than 85 percent of its 121,600 square miles (about the size of West and East Germany combined) stands higher than 4000 feet. Nearly 1¼ million people live in the State, and unlike Texas very few of them are of Mexican descent. The State was captured in 1846 after the Mexican wars, when the local population was evacuated southwards.

The capital, Santa Fe, is one of the oldest cities in America, settled by the Spanish in 1610. It was not until 302 years had passed that it became capital of newly constituted New Mexico. It is fairly small, with about 40,000 people, living in a colourful city where adobe buildings (even an adobe capitol – or at least intended to look like one – which is circular and simple, just two storeys built in 1966) abound. It was an important marker on the Santa Fe Trail of old, but the city, although embraced in the title of the greatest long distance railroad in America – the Atchison, Topeka and Santa Fe – is 27 miles distant from the tracks, the stop for the capital being at Lamy, with small buses meeting trains.

Albuquerque, 60 miles to the Southwest and a major division point on the Santa Fe Railroad, is by far the largest city in New Mexico, with 300,000 people. It is on the Rio Grande, no longer a border river at this point but still a significant stream. AMTRAK's "South West Chief" serves the city and picks up an Indian guide for its onward journeyings through fabulous Indian country "where desert winds carve steeples to the sky". There are vast Indian Reservations all over New Mexico, those of the Navajo and Apache being the largest. Albuquerque was named in 1706 for the Spanish Ducal Viceroy.

High mountains, plateaux, and forests

mark the northern part of New Mexico, while the South is largely desert. Nights are cool to cold, the days brilliantly sunny and crisp; many people with asthma and other breathing problems retire here, but altitude can increase heart attacks and complexions get dried out. Wheeler Peak near Indian-oriented Taos in the North of the State, is the highest, more than 13,000 feet.

The Southwest is real Western country, mostly extreme desert but with giant buttes rearing to the sky. The Southeast is raw land yet it contains the prime tourist attraction, Carlsbad Caverns, a National Park with about four miles of deep caves below the Guadeloupe Mountains. Nearby is the Living Desert State Park.

In all the 200 miles from El Paso to the Arizona border there are only three towns, one of them – Las Cruces – of significant size with a university, the other two – Deming (pronounced Deaming) and Lordsburg just hamlets, really, but famed in the history of the West, stage stops on the Butterfield route, and Hollywood movies.

Arizona

Arizona contains the Big One, the greatest geographical attraction in the world, a mighty cleft in the earth made by the Colorado River. The Grand Canyon is 217 miles long, from five to 13 miles wide, and 4,000 to 5,500 feet deep. Descriptions are ineffective; it must be seen, and especially at sunset. It is a National Park and there are lodges, while sightseeing helicopters can be taken, at some cost. It can also be entered, on muleback, by fit tourists undertaking a two-day trek to the Sunset Ranch and back. Millions of people a year just come to gaze from its Arizona rim, far fewer from

the higher and more remote North rim. It is hot by day in summer, bitter in winter, and always chilly at night, sometimes very cold indeed during winter dawns (below zero in fact).

Renting a car is the easiest way and there are rim-bay parkings but buses galore go there from Flagstaff and Williams, while a train service (first put on by the Santa Fe in 1900) has been restored from Williams Junction, using steam locomotives of modern type, two of them purchased new from China. The Arizona side has an airport, with services from Las Vegas as well as sightseeing flights (no longer allowed to fly below the canyon rims).

Arizona was the last of the 48 States of mainland America to be admitted to the Union. That was on February 14, 1912, just five weeks after New Mexico. Prior to those dates, both were wide open Territories, governed from Washington, with overall law applied by Federal Marshals. They were the last vestiges of the Old West beloved of Hollywood for so many years and shown in literally thousands of movies, some great epics, most second runs.

Well populated by West standards, Arizona is expanding with people coming to the Valley of the Sun in the huge Phoenix area for retirement in a hot dry climate. Well over 2½ million live in the State, a third of them in Greater Phoenix, but it is quite a large State with 114,000 square miles – about equal to Italy. Unusually, the largest city is also the capital, where the State House is comparatively small topped by a dome made of tufa stone from Arizona's Skull Valley. Scottsdale is the ultra modern suburb where 100,000 people live.

Tucson is the second city with nearly 300,000 people, risen from an old Wild

West town (there is a section known as Old Tucson complete with shoot-outs). The city is pronounced Tew-sonn. Like Phoenix, it is on the 'Sunset Limited' route to Los Angeles, while Highway 10 passes through both cities almost parallel to the railroad. Nogales is the most southerly city, right on the Mexican border facing a smaller Mexican city of the same name.

Very large and increasing numbers of foreign tourists are visiting Arizona, not only for the Grand Canyon but for other attractions and, of course, the guaranteed sunshine. Some are even devoted to it in high summer when the temperature is over 100 degrees. Phoenix can be counted on to have a daytime maximum of over 90 degrees from mid-May to late September. But winter nights can be cold even at Tucson and on the high plateau to the North heavy snow can lay for weeks, in exceptional years of high precipitation.

A vast natural wonder of the high plateau on the Arizona-Utah border is Monument Valley. It is on Navajo Indian land, stretching for 45 miles along the only highway (163 into Utah). There are hundreds of incredibly eroded buttes, some gigantic, others small. Monument Valley has been the background to many movies including "Stage Coach" and to many advertisements.

Lake Havasu City brings thousands of Britons on their travels for here, across an arm of two artificial lakes, stands the original London Bridge of 1840. It was moved and re-assembled stone by stone. There is no truth whatsoever in the legend that the buyer thought he was getting the Tower Bridge – he was a Scotsman quite familiar with the Thames.

Around the Bridge are numerous relics of pre-war London from red buses to shops.

Unless on a bus tour it is virtually essential to drive a rental car, and if coming up from the Colorado River crossing near Blythe, California, on the direct secondary road, care must be taken. It runs for 47 miles through the Reservation of the Colorado River Indians and they are unfriendly to strays from the road. This highway is also subject to flash-floods if there is heavy rain in the North of the State; check weather reports.

Southern California

Crossing from Arizona into California the stark desert does not change and it must have been hard for the early pioneers to believe they had reached the land of promise. But this vast State has room to embrace everything a settler could want and still leave half its area to barren, arid wilderness. California has 43 named mountain ranges as well as the famed Sierra Nevadas. It has more sand desert than the Kalahari. As for its economic success, its gross national product would put it – if it were a nation in its own right – in eighth place in the world.

They call it the 'Golden State' with good reason (the Gold Rush of 1849 populated it). With 158,000 square miles it is the third in size in the Union, one and a half times the size of New Zealand. We are concerned in this chapter with Southern California (the northern parts are dealt with in Chapter Ten). For all practical visitor purposes, this means Los Angeles and San Diego. It means Hollywood, Palm Springs, the Sequoia National Park, Mount Whitney (14,495 feet and highest in mainland America), King's Canyon National Park, and to the

North of that the greatest scenic area in the West, Yosemite National Park.

Los Angeles

To reach the amazing urban and suburban spread of humanity 16 million strong and fifty miles across which comprises Greater Los Angeles, one must cross one of two passes if coming from the East, in fact, other than making a coastal approach. The Southern Pacific tracks, and the train "Sunset Limited" whose journey we have followed from Texas, plus Highway 10, come over the San Gorgonio Pass 2612 feet. Only a relatively few miles to the East they had been deep below sea level, where the Salton Sea is 235 feet below. Both Union Pacific and Santa Fe, whose tracks carry the "Desert Wind" and the "South West Chief", plus Highway 15 from Las Vegas, approach over the Cajon Pass, at 4259 feet.

It is because the over inhabited sprawl of the great city is shut in on all sides but the West by high mountain ranges that the infamous smog builds up, its effects worsened by nearly 16 million road vehicles. The natural air conditioning of the sea and its breezes keep the Angelenos cool EXCEPT on those fortunately rare occasions when the Santa Anna wind comes in over the passes and this hot dry terror heats things up to unbearable levels.

It is often said that everyone needs 'wheels of their own' for getting around Los Angeles. The world's earliest Freeway system, some of the elevated highways now getting a bit worn after 35 years, certainly speed up road travel except during clogs – and these are frequent in rush periods. But it is no longer true, no matter how vigorously Angelenos may claim the need for cars. A new Metro and a greatly expanded bus network have changed things.

Once, until 1960–62, there was a splendid electric trolley system called Pacific Electric, which went nearly everywhere, often fast. It was buried under the weight of oil-inspired Freeways, but these sweeping concrete networks – although still intensively used – have gone out of fashion in their turn. As yet the costly new Metro runs only on one route but will soon extend widely. Meanwhile, RTD (Rapid Transit District of Southern California) has built up its bus fleet from a miserable minimum of 350 aged vehicles in 1970 (when they used to claim you died of heat exhaustion waiting for a bus) to more than 3300 today. The service is good and relatively cheap – every two minutes on Wilshire Boulevard, five minutes on Sunset, every half an hour on outer journeys such as expresses to Long Beach. Some buses run all night. A new light rail transit system now runs to Long Beach, opened in 1990.

Visitors from outside California can buy RTD bus passes at very favourable rates from booths in Downtown (Union Station has one). They are good for two days, five days, or a week and also allow discounts at certain stores and restaurants. Express buses to Los Angeles International Airport (known generally as LAX) are covered, so are the shuttle buses Downtown and around the Airport terminals. You can use them for trips to Hollywood's Universal studios and to Long Beach (32 miles) to see "Queen Mary" and the adjoining "Spruce Goose" (largest plane ever built).

S. Californian Beaches

The beaches of the Pacific Ocean are world famous, such as Malibu, Santa Monica, and Venice (the 'Way-out' seaside where roller skating is the rage and physical pursuits of all kinds take place), The ocean is about 12 miles from Downtown measured at City Hall. One beach is named after Will Rogers.

Wonderful beaches with good surfing extend all the way South to San Diego, the big city 128 miles from the centre of 'L.A.'. They face the so called Gulf of Santa Catalina (the ferries to popular restful Santa Catalina Island make their 25 mile trips from Long Beach and Newport Beach) and include San Clemente, Carlsbad, and the cluster around Oceanside like Cardiff-by-the-Sea.

The climate of San Diego, pure Mediterranean type but better than found adjoining that sea, is regarded by many as the best in the world. The city is interesting and healthy without L.A.'s excesses. It is reached by car in 2½ hours by the San Diego Freeway or up to 10 times daily in the same time by AMTRAK trains.

The world's finest Zoo is here; the "Star of India" ship museum, Old San Diego State Historical Park, Sea World at Mission Bay Park, the Old Globe Theatre (for Shakespeare), are among other attractions in this city of 850,000 people. Its urban public transportation is cheap and efficient, and do not miss a ride on the 'Red Trolleys', actually super-trams built in Dusseldorf, Germany, which maintain a frequent service for a Dollar to Tijuana 20 miles to the South and just across the border into Mexico.

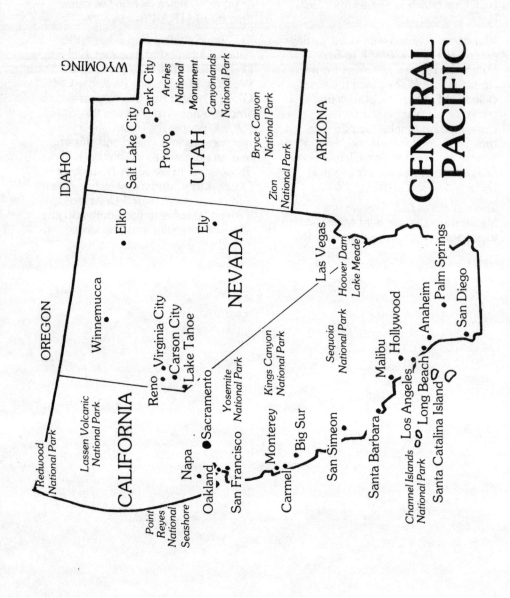

CENTRAL
PACIFIC

10. Central Pacific

Nevada, Western Utah, Northern California

Background

The name Central Pacific was given to the western part of the Trans-Continental Railroad which was thrust across the nation from 1863 to 1869. It refers to the section from Promontory in Utah, where the eastern and western sections met, to San Franciso Bay. This chapter takes a broader view, covering the central and northern parts of California, the State of Nevada, and western Utah from Salt Lake City.

Four of the most important tourist cities lie in the Central Pacific region, places which bring international visitors on a large scale. They are San Francisco, Las Vegas, Reno, and Salt Lake City. San Francisco has always been a popular destination and is often spoken of as 'Everyone's Favourite City', but Salt Lake is new on the tourist circuit, mainly because of the wonderful winter ski areas high in the Wasatch Mountains behind and above the city. As for Las Vegas, it is new by any standards, having been discovered as a watering hole for Union Pacific trains in 1906. Not until the late 1940's did any of the amazing expansion and vigour begin to appear. Reno became famous in the late 1930's when it was the centre for 'quickie' divorces emanating from Hollywood (and elsewhere). The title "Biggest Little City in the World" – still printed in huge letters on a banner across the main street – was bestowed on it, by itself, in 1932.

Sierra Nevada

Central Pacific's crowning glory are the Sierra Nevada Mountains, snow-capped all year round and rising to 13,145 feet with some severe and notorious high passes. The mountains sprawl, North to South, roughly marking the territorial boundaries between Nevada and California.

It was on the Donner Pass in 1840, at an elevation of 7135 feet that the Donner emigrant party in their covered wagons became snowed in for the winter, whereupon they turned cannibal. This is one of the grimmest stories of the great emigration trails, but few people know that exactly a century later there was another case of cannibalism on the Donner. A Southern Pacific train was totally snowed in, and lay unrelieved for eight days, causing one or two murders as food ran out (together with heat) and the eating of corpses.

The Sierras are wonderful for skiing at safe and marked sites, and they are wonderful in summer for hiking and cool camping. But they can be dangerous and local knowledge should always be sought if crossing by car. Sonora Pass, Tioga Pass, Ebbetts Pass, and Carson Pass are closed in winter, and that may mean until May.

To the East the Sierras fall away into high desert which is the northern part of the State of Nevada. It is on this high ground that Reno is situated, a cool dry place rapidly expanding as a gambling resort rivalling its hotter southern sister, Las Vegas. The railway, once Central Pacific and now Southern Pacific (with AMTRAK passenger trains), still runs through the main street.

Nevada

Nevada was founded by Spanish explorers, searching as always for gold, which in this instance they found, together with a great deal of silver. The word means 'snow covered', a true state of affairs looking westwards to the high mountains, but the semi-arid nature of Reno and the small cluster of towns to the East of it rarely have heavy falls of snow. Attending the big annual Air Show at Reno one September, we were sweltering in 90 degrees, but next day a bitter wind blew off the Sierras and snow began falling heavily!

Elko and Sparks are the towns to the East, which began life on the new railway, as crew division points and marshalling yards. Water supplies were all-important in steam days, found here in abundant deep wells. There is a major visitor attraction in Sparks, only about five miles from the centre of Reno, called Harrahs, a gigantic motorcar museum belonging to the former owner of a major hotel and gambling resort. In addition to rank after rank of veteran and vintage cars there are some early aircraft.

High in the mountains South of Reno are two historic (by Nevada standards) small cities, Carson City, the Capital, (named after pioneer Kit Carson) and Virginia City, the community which grew up around the silver and mining camps. One of the smallest capitals in the Union, Carson City is close to the shores of

magnificent Lake Tahoe, a vast natural lake shared between California and Nevada. It is a popular ski area in winter, and a cool paradise in summer. It first came into prominence when it was chosen as the location for the Jeannette MacDonald–Nelson Eddy movie "Rose Marie" in 1936.

Carson City's State House has a silver dome, the only one so coated in the United States. The glint of this dome can be seen a dozen miles away at even higher Virginia City, and appropriately there is a community in between called Silver City. Running in this area is the restored Virginia and Truckee Railroad, which did not close as a public service until the late 1960's. It uses vintage steam locomotives and elderly rolling stock on its scenic standard gauge track. Virginia City is mostly a living museum these days, restored bars from the days of the Comstock Lode silver wealth lining the steep main street. Historic recipes from the time of Kit Carson are served in jazzed-up cafes.

Nevada is about 500 miles from North to South and some 320 miles from West to East, and that encompasses a big area, bigger than Italy (minus Sicily). So there is room enough for many spacious things, and one of these is Nellis Air Force Base and Nuclear Testing Range. There is also Indian Springs Gunnery Range. Visitors do not, as a very strict rule, enter these zones which cover a total area considerably larger than Denmark. But there is vast roaming territory for the herds of wild mustangs. Dotted all over Nevada are ghost towns, some of which have become tourist attractions, where silver and gold miners tried and mostly failed to find a fortune. Cherry Creek near Caliente on the main line of the Union Pacific–AMTRAK railroad line from Salt Lake City to Las Vegas, is one that is looked after, with guides.

But if driving through Nevada and happening upon a ghost town on a minor road, the experience is fascinating, perhaps eerie, as the desert wind flaps broken shutters, slams a door, or raises dust devils. There is silence, and a feeling of recent history more appreciated than if being guided in a group through a patched-up ghost town. But take great care, if coming in from hot sunlight to a ruined shack or saloon – there may be rattlesnakes around.

Nevada has space in plenty for Indian Reservations, like the Walker River through which the State Highway 95 passes. It is not considered a good thing to stop and get out of a car with a camera. There are danger zones, too, areas away from roads in most cases but close to them in a few instances. These are usually military secret spots, missile bases or air stations.

Travelling East from the developed Reno/Sparks region along Highway 95, or on the Southern Pacific/AMTRAK railroad line which parallels it (although the tracks were there 80 years before the road came as a metalled strip), we pass through mountainous desert to Winnemucca. This small town was named after the Chief of the Piute tribe, a man who always believed Indians and white people could live in peace together.

It is on the Humboldt River, whose drainage gives some pasture to the otherwise dry country. High mountains are on either side, including Sonoma Peak, 9395 feet, and North Peak, 8550 feet. The small town of Battle Mountain commemorates a fierce clash between Nevada pioneers and Piutes in 1857, a few years before

Chief Winnemucca took over.

Both rail and highway follow the Humboldt through Elko (population 7,600 and the biggest in the East of the State). Soon afterwards the giant of the East Humboldt Range looms up, "Hole in the Mountain" Peak, 11,267 feet. Rail and road part company at tiny Wells, the former heading for the Great Salt Lake of Utah, while the highway, renumbered 93A and then 80 as it crosses into Utah, strikes across the Great Salt Lake Desert. This is a stark endless land of white sandy salt glaring in the sun.

Western Utah

The Great Salt Lake itself, a vast expanse of shimmering densely salty water 1438 square miles in area, lies about three quarters of a mile above sea level. On its flats racing cars and motorbikes have established world speed records. The lake is shallow.

Using this shallowness, the main line of the Southern Pacific takes a short cut across it by means of a lengthy causeway. Originally, back in 1869, the Union Pacific and Southern Pacific's forerunner – Central Pacific – went around it, to meet at Promontory Point, Utah. This is now a National Monument, containing replicas of the original locomotives plus a museum depicting the events of the Golden Spike which completed the first Trans Continental railroad (apart from Panama).

The tall tower of the Church of the Latter Day Saints office building can be seen as one approaches the western side of Salt Lake City, and on a hilltop the magnificent dome of the State Capitol of Brigham Young's city. The spires of the Temple, forbidden to non-Mormons, can soon be seen. More than half a million people live in this clean, sprawling city with its backdrop of snow covered mountains. Just 36 miles to the North is Ogden, Utah, with 70,000 people, still a major railroad centre but with only one passenger train a day, the "Pioneer". To the Southeast of Salt Lake City lies Provo, with 54,000 people, where the Mormon University is located, a seat of learning noted for extreme neatness of dress and strict discipline.

These three cities of West Utah hold considerably more than half the total population of the enormous State, where wilderness and some of the most astounding high rock scenery in the world hold sway.

That important Nevada Highway 95 which I mentioned passes through Lathrop Wells on its way to Las Vegas. This is scarcely a place to stop but it is a road junction with lesser road Number 29 signposted Amargosa (Death Valley Junction). Most visitors to this desert-mountain region of America want to have a look at fearsome Death Valley. Some people, particularly the late Leslie Halliwell, author of so many film reference books before his death in 1989, love the place. Others fear it. It must not be entered by inexperienced travellers using just one car between June and September, otherwise its name could well have dreadful significance. It is the hottest place on Earth, and reaches down to 282 feet below sea level, the lowest in the world apart from the Dead Sea. The bare high rocky mountains surrounding the valley radiate the sun's heat, and the highest recorded temperature of 138 degrees Fahrenheit (59 degrees Celsius) was IN THE SHADE and there is precious little of that. What water seen to be lying about is bad water. But Scotty's Castle is a tourist sight to see, and a visit with a Valley drive (the car must

be air-conditioned with spare water) is first rate in Oct–May.

Actually there are a lot of myths associated with Death Valley. Apart from summer it is not a dangerous place to visit, and indeed it is a National Monument covering some 3000 square miles. Walter Scotty's 'Castle' (he built this with monies earned working with Buffalo Bill's Wild West Show) gets as many as 100,000 visitors a season. Anyone going in with a tour or with a private car should try to reach Dante's View, an observation point where you can see, at one and the same time, the lowest point on the American Continent and the highest point – Mount Whitney, 14,494 feet. But always remember that the Indian name for the valley is Tomesha, which means 'red hot earth'.

Las Vegas

About 135 miles away from the Amargosa road junction are the outskirts of the fastest growing desert city in the world, Las Vegas. It is not only the gambling 'capital of the World' but the world's top entertainment city. In 1990 the population was approaching 600,000, ten times what it was when I attended a Convention there in 1962. Its spectacular hotels, many of them the largest of their kind anywhere, stretch now into areas which were total desert less than 30 years ago.

A totally artificial place, Las Vegas grew rapidly from 1946 onwards, the year in which Union Pacific Railroad President F. A. Ashby created a 'resort concept' following the replacement of steam traction by diesels. This led to a loss of over a thousand jobs as the need for water declined and locomotive sheds were closed. The State of Nevada's gambling laws, applied to Reno and that part of Lake Tahoe in Nevada, helped the fledgling Las Vegas. From two hotels the resort expanded to 200 inside 15 years. The big ones all had show theatres behind their gaming halls. Huge profits enabled big names to be attracted at fees Broadway and Hollywood could only marvel at. The trend has continued, and within a few years several hotels of 500 or more rooms will have theatres paying top stars a million Dollars a week.

The legal gambling in Las Vegas is not one-sided. Some 46 in every 100 persons visiting the city come away winners. The 54 who lose contribute hundreds of millions of Dollars a week to the place. Best prospects of a win are in the cheaper downtown casinos on Fremont Street leading away from the Union Pacific Plaza built above the AMTRAK station. The slot machines (there are over two million of these in Nevada) taking 25 cents coins pay out 97 percent of receipts.

Very low costs are a feature of Las Vegas. Hotel charges are less than half those in major cities across the nation, while cafes and restaurants are extremely cheap. Breakfasts for less than a Dollar are advertised on hoardings. Meals in casinos are priced in single figures, massive steak dinners, for instance, at under $5.

There are no clocks in Las Vegas. The city is open 24 hours a day, and in the small hours of the morning, from a vantage point on a hillside when the traffic is light, it is reputed that the low roar of tens of thousands of slot machine handles being pulled sounds across the desert!

Local transportation is a disaster. Once adequate for 50,000 people, it is hopeless for twelve times that number. Buses run up and down the 'Strip' every 15 minutes, packed tight, and charging a Dollar. Taxis are not easy to find and they, too, charge a lot. In fact, transport is the only costly and inadequate item in the place. But they are still talking, even hopefully, about a monorail system and a very high speed rail link to Los Angeles. Meanwhile, there is one passenger train each way daily ("Desert Wind"), several Greyhound buses, and a large number of aircraft from McCarren Airport.

The 'Strip' and off-streets are jammed with private cars, which can all be parked safely in the giant car parks of the hotels but once taken on the roads, get nowhere fast and find no on-street parking Downtown. Some of the hotel car parks are so large they have been used for Formula One motor racing circuits!

One of the greatest man-made sights in America lies just 40 miles from Las Vegas, spanning the Nevada–Arizona border. This is the Hoover Dam, which used to be called Boulder Dam, across the Colorado River. Tours are made for visitors, with coaches from Las Vegas every day, and tourists may enter the spillways. It ranks with Grand Coulee Dam in Washington State as the largest in the nation, and its 726 feet high concrete face is the highest in the world, backing up so much water that Lake Meade, formed behind it, gives a veritable 'sea' for Las Vegas's aquatic pleasures – it has 550 miles of shoreline.

Las Vegas rightly belongs to the 'Great South West' but because Nevada's wider parts fit into Central Pacific I have included the city in this chapter. Without Vegas, Nevada would sink back to desert poverty, now that virtually all the silver that once kept it above the breadline has been mined.

Southern California

Crossing the Sierra we descend towards the lush warm lands where the American and Sacramento Rivers join. This was the target of so many thousands of hopeful immigrants in their wagon trains, sunny and peaceful, a region where almost everything would grow. The city they built at the river junciton, where a tiny Spanish mission existed and some gold miners' camps lay scattered, was called Sacramento and became capital of the State of California on admission to the Union in 1850. Today it has a population of about a quarter of a million, enjoying great prosperity.

The elegant Capitol building has a splendid dome, which was coated in 22 carat gold for the 1776–1976 celebrations but has now gone back to bronze (the gold scraped off?). The city has a brand new tram service using German equipment, which has transformed the local transportation. A feature of Sacramento is the wonderful California Railway Museum, housing many locomotives which were used in the State, with rolling stock, suitable sounds and visual displays, and railroad experiences, such as the occupancy of a sleeping car from the 1930's with motion and extraneous noises. Engines from the Museum come out and haul trains for tourists over a five mile track beside the Sacramento River.

A restored part of town called 'Old Sacramento' is well done, with a dozen authentic restaurants from the past open for business. The views on warm summer evenings, while dining, are attractive, although there are no hills in the vicinity. A very clear early spring day, though, puts the snow-capped Sierras in view.

San Francisco/S. California

It is 90 miles going Westsouthwest to San Francisco, but if driving, a detour to the Napa Valley is worthy. This is the famous wine-making valley where the best California whites and reds are produced. Tastings at various wineries are freely arranged, but on a hot day – and it can get very hot in summer in the Napa – the most refreshing thing to do is to enjoy a meal outside with a half gallon of chilled light white wine. Prices are extraordinarily modest, but one should not expect the best Napa Valley wines to be cheap. They have a world wide reputation these days and it must not be forgotten (by Francophiles) that after the phylloxia disease killed so many French vineyards after the turn of the century, they were all replanted by healthy grapes from the Napa Valley.

San Francisco is almost an island, reached by bridges and ferries except from the South. Oakland is an equally large city across the Bay, terminus of the trans-Continental railway line. Since the mid 1970's, BART has made travel extremely easy and fast on this high speed regional railway system which goes underground through San Francisco and Oakland. BART stands for Bay Area Regional Transport; it is clean, speedy, modern and cheap.

The city itself has, like Seattle, all forms of public transport with the famous Cable Cars the best known. There are normal trams both above and below ground, trolley buses, diesel buses, and ferries (once virtually extinguished but now restored in part due to over-use of the Golden Gate Bridge, called the 'Car Strangled Spanner'). MUNI is the name given to transport except for BART, and fixed prices are low, while senior citizens, no matter where their place of origin, pay only 20 cents.

Only an experienced motorist with local knowledge would try to drive a car around San Francisco, where the hills are so steep people can barely walk up them without handrails. There are special restrictions on parking in hilly areas, and on making turns. But the three Cable Car routes take care of the worst hills, the ancient (but greatly restored) vehicles running at 9½ miles an hour up or down the hills, their 'gripman' visibly working his machine grasping the underground cable. These cars have been declared the only 'National Moving Monuments' in the USA. To ride them costs one Dollar, but locals can buy sheets of commuter tickets at a much lower rate. There is a Cable Car Museum where the three routes join on Mason Street; it is free to visitors.

Not to be missed in the city is the developing Maritime Museum with old ferries and coastal ships, the square rigger "Balcutha" berthed near equally interesting Fisherman's Wharf (numerous fish restaurants, no longer cheap), the Ferry Building near the Bay Bridge, only large building to have survived the 1906 earthquake and fire, and a drink at the 'Top of the Mark' (Mark Hopkins Hotel) for the view – no longer the high point but still good and traditional.

San Francisco has had two major earthquakes from its proximity to the San Andreas faultline, in 1906 and 1989, but it is often rocked slightly, sometimes even five times in a day. It is not normally alarming and usually causes no damage – there are no chimney pots or excrescences on buildings to fall off.

Going North across the Golden Gate Bridge (toll for drivers one way only) you are soon in the Redwood Empire, the great green glory of the Central Pacific. For hundreds of miles the giant Sequoia trees – the world's oldest living things apart from Nevada's Bristlecone Pines – dominate the hilly landscape. Some stand over 300 feet high and one has a 'tunnel' cut through it in a park area. The Sequoias – Redwoods – are regenerating and are still logged commercially except where large stands have been preserved, usually bearing a donor's name.

Going South, the only way out of the city not requiring a bridge, one soon enters Silicon Valley, with the cities of San Jose and Santa Clara full of ultra-modern factories. A tremendous thing to do Southwest of San Jose is to ride the "Roaring Camp and Big Trees" logging railway, a preserved tourist line using all three types of special logging geared steam engines. There is an extension now to the boardwalk of Santa Cruz, a popular Pacific holiday spot.

Finally, slightly further South, there is the Monterey Peninsula, (John Steinbeck Country), with the arty town of Carmel and an area so secluded they charge two dollars just to drive round. "We try to keep the United States out" say the residents . . .

11. Pacific North West

Washington, Oregon, Idaho

Background

Magnificently scenic and cool, washed by the waters of the Pacific Ocean and backed by deep green forests rising to high volcanic mountains, the States of Oregon and Washington are new territory by global standards. Sydney, Australia, was almost ninety years old when the first settlers came to Seattle, now the biggest city of the Pacific North West. The Oregon Trail was a spin-off from the well beaten overland routes to California, and its first travellers made the difficult journey a century after the Spanish were well established in what became the Golden State.

Early explorers had found no gold on the North Pacific shore, and the Spanish felt it too cool and wet for settlement. Two American soldiers, Captain Meriwether Lewis and Captain William Clark, were despatched by President Jefferson to explore the Pacific North West in 1804. They set out from St Louis on the Missouri River on May 14 of that year and got back safely on September 23, 1806. The Lewis and Clark Expedition is rated as the opening of America's greatest wilderness, and they were the first white men to reach the Pacific from inland at those latitudes. Captain Vancouver of the British Navy had seen it from the sea a few years earlier, and two cities bear his name in consequence, the larger one in British Columbia, Canada, and the smaller one on the Columbia River where it marks the border between Washington and Oregon.

The main reason why Lewis and Clark were sent off on their remarkable journey of discovery was that the fledgling United States had bought the territory the year before from the French! This was the Louisiana Purchase of 1803, covering some 827,000 square miles reaching from the Mississippi shores in Louisiana to the North West. No one knew anything about it and the French certainly had no intention of settling or administering it.

Reports brought back showed that all this was wonderful country, with fertile valleys and rich forests, particularly so as the Pacific Ocean was approached. The Indians encountered were said to be mainly friendly and helpful; in fact, Sacajawea, an Indian woman, acted as guide for Lewis and Clark during much of their journey. It would seem that the youthful Uncle Sam's payment of just 15 million Dollars to Emperor Napoleon of France had been a bargain even allowing for the prices of those days – under 20 Dollars per square mile!

There were no waves of emigrants to the Pacific North West, only a few loggers and fishermen. A sawmill on Puget Sound was established in 1852 and with the friendly aid of an Indian chief named Sealth a community called Duwamps prospered. By the

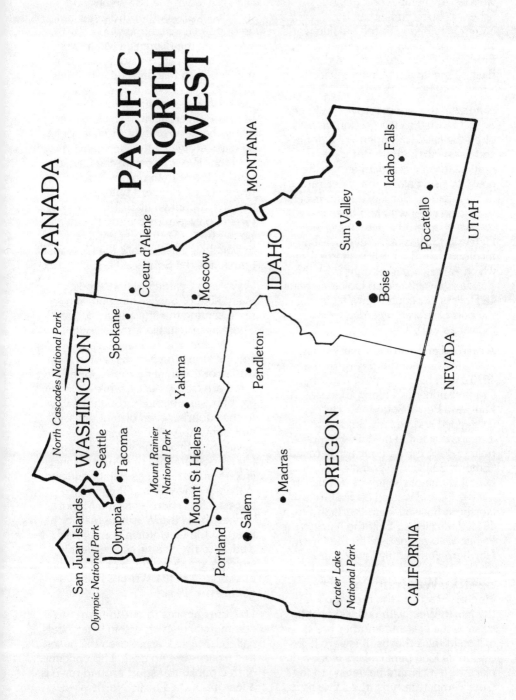

1870's Duwamps was a fairly large wooden township with outlying fisheries. Such contact as the community had with the outside world was by coastal paddle steamer to San Francisco. This city was linked to the East by the famous Union Pacific Trans-continental railroad in 1869.

Naturally, the wooden town on Puget Sound burned to the ground, as was often the case with open fires, drink, and flimsy structures. But it was rebuilt, sturdily and with stone, the new city rising along the waterfront being renamed Seattle in honour of the Indian chief who had been so helpful. It entered a new phase as the Gateway to Alaska, an even vaster territory than the Louisiana Purchase, which America had bought from the Russians for 7.2 million Dollars, at only 12 Dollars per square mile (even so, the purchase was regarded as 'Seward's Folly').

A railroad entrepreneur named Jim Hill came on the scene early in the 1870's with his concept of a northern Trans-continental linking Chicago, St Paul, and Puget Sound. Mr Hill succeeded and became known as the 'Empire Builder'. The daily Superliner train making the 44 hour trip is called "Empire Builder" to commemorate him. It is one of the ten best trains in the world, and was so on his Great Northern Railway from the 1930's to 1971. Jim Hill also built the Northern Pacific Railway, parallel to the Great Northern at a slightly lower latitude.

Seattle/Washington

Modern Seattle is the metropolis of the North West with 600,000 people living in the city and another half a million in the suburbs. It is very high-rise on its long peninsula, a work-a-day place with a climate belonging to the Cool Temperate type, the same as southern England. There is a lot of rain, but when the sun shines and there is clear weather the vistas are among the finest in the world. To the West rear the Olympian Mountains, always snow-capped, some of them unclimbed to this day and with a few deep valleys not yet fully surveyed. To the East the local 'hausmountain' is Mount Rainier, giant of the Cascades, whose cone rises to 14,410 feet, only 30 miles away. To the Northeast there is Mount Baker, close to the Canadian border, lower than Rainier (this is pronounced 'Reneer') but still a massive mountain at 10,107 feet. Green, hilly islands dot the Puget Sound to the Southwest and high Snoqualmie Pass across the Cascades dominates the Southeast vista.

Visitors to Seattle will find almost every kind of public transport at a low price serving the city and its suburbs. There are Australian trams bought from Melbourne running a frequent service along the two miles of waterfront. On many routes in the city there are trolley buses, while ordinary diesel buses operate through the city to the suburbs, even distant ones. A new subway system is being developed. From the waterfront large ferries operate into the Puget Sound, linking islands such as Bainbridge and Whidbey – Seattle has the nation's largest fleet. There is even a Monorail service, from the Westlake Mall in the heart of the Downtown commercial district to the Seattle Space Needle which rears above the Seattle Center built up out of the World's Fair complex of 1964.

Low cost applies to outside the commercial district; within what locals call the 'Magic Carpet' area the buses and trolleys are *no cost*. This concept of free public transport around town is a feature of the Pacific North West cities and will be found in Tacoma, Washington, and also Portland, Oregon. It cuts out car clogging and parking congestion. If you take a bus beyond the limits you merely drop the appropriate coinage (65 cents at the time of writing) into a glass box beside the driver, when leaving the vehicle.

Ferry rides are not particularly cheap but they offer a wonderful sea trip amid some of the world's most scenic waters. To Bremerton, the big naval base up the Sinclair Inlet, the trip takes an hour and costs about five and a half dollars, but it shows splendid views (on a clear day, naturally) of the Olympic Peninsula and the Hood Canal. This, and other ferry trips from Seattle's Colman Dock, is often used by local people as well as visitors for picnics.

Longer ferry trips can be made to Port Angeles (on the Olympic Peninsula) and up the coast to Victoria in Canada. The latter can be made as a round trip lasting from eight in the morning until ten at night (with five hours ashore on this most English of Canada's cities) at a cost of under 30 dollars.

Most coastal ferries take cars for very little more than the passenger fare. The hard-working "Coho" of Black Ball Line runs the 20 miles from Port Angeles across the Straits of Juan de Fuca to Victoria charging just 25 dollars for car and driver, with another five dollars for an extra passenger. English Channel ferries out of Dover for France charge eight times that amount, and they boast of extra revenue from duty free shops!

Ferries are worth stressing on the Pacific North West. They are value for money, comfortable and scenic – try the San Juan Islands all day trip out of Anacortes for about 12 Dollars.

Gazing in any direction, whether from the top of the Space Needle, or from the waterfront (appropriately named these days 'Alaska Way' although part of it was the infamous 'Skid Row' of Depression times), it is easy to see why Seattle is called "The Emerald City".

But it is not all shipping, lumber and commerce. To many millions of people around the world it means Boeing. The giant aircraft construction works at Everett, ten miles North of the city, cover nearly a thousand acres. Free tours are arranged and guides show visitors around the actual plant turning out jets, as well as showing both technical and amusing films. This is one of the biggest manufacturing sites in the world while the covered building is the largest by volume in the world. Yet there are other Boeing plants scattered around the outskirts of Seattle, including one turning out Vertol trams (which Americans call electric trolleys) and Jetfoil craft, although less than twenty of the latter have been built, mostly now working out of Hong Kong or Dover (for Ostend).

Quite new is Seattle's Museum of Flight, on East Marginal Way, using the original 1916 hangar of the fledgling Boeing Company. This is being expanded and is housed partly in a six storey glass and steel gallery. There may be a nominal charge when the full Museum is functioning but at present visitors are welcome to a free unguided tour.

Other Washington
To go inland really calls for a rental car, especially if the Cascades are to be seen or crossed. Snoqualmie Pass is a great place to reach, but almost as spectacular are the Snoqualmie Falls, well short of the Pass, where a

preserved steam railway using some fascinating locomotives runs several miles to a bridge over the Falls.

The big city to the East is Spokane, 'capital of the Inland Empire'. Three important railway routes came together here in the early 1880's, and it is today a junction where the AMTRAK superliner "Empire Builder" splits to serve Seattle and Portland. Like so many early wooden cities it was burned to the ground. That was in 1889 but the rebuilding work by architect Kirtland Cutter has resulted in some of the finest structures in the nation, especially along West Riverside Avenue.

Unlike the coastal cities, Spokane has extremes of climate with a severe winter. It was one of the first cities to have indoor shopping, no less than two miles of second storey passageways in the downtown area linking department stores. There are great ski areas a few miles from the city, one of them called "49 Degrees North" which means it is close to the Canadian border.

Two outstanding places to see in the 325 miles between Seattle and Spokane are Ellensburg and the Grand Coulee Dam. Ellensburg is a genuine cow-town, famed for its rodeos, but it is also a college community around Central Washington University. It is on the eastern slopes of the Cascade Range, astride the Yakima River on which there are raft and float trips to be made through splendid gorges close to town.

The Yakima Valley at a lower altitude produces some very good wine indeed with some fifteen wineries open for tours and tastings. This is probably the furthest north wine producing region in the United States, but it is beginning to rival California's more famous Napa Valley.

The Grand Coulee Dam is on the mighty Columbia River and is the largest in North America. It was finished in 1941 and claims to be the largest structure on Earth, with miles of concrete on a vast scale. The spillway of the dam is twice the height of Niagara. Free self-guided tours are available.

Anyone getting this far might like to see a somewhat crazy windmill collection at North Dam Park, set up by eccentric Emil Gehrke, who invented things, but did these odd-looking windmills just for fun.

The States of Washington and Oregon are becoming famous for beer. Dozens of small breweries are to be found tucked away in valleys, on the edges of towns, and on the banks of the Yakima River. They are known as microbreweries, using pure Pacific North West water, and the result is real ale. This product has several times won the International Beer Exhibition top award at Brighton in England. Try Grants (from Yakima), whose malty Scottish Ale has a reputation worldwide. These beers from the North West have no relationship with the widely drunk slightly gassy products from Milwaukee.

Oregan/Idaho

If Seattle is the Emerald City, Portland, Oregon, is the City of Roses. They thrive in its pleasant climate, which is slightly warmer than that of Seattle, yet part of the Cool Temperate type with adequate rain and little winter frost. In late May and June, Portland's 138 parks are ablaze with roses.

Sometimes known as the 'smallest Big

City on the West Coast', Portland is on the Willamette River while its outskirts are also on the Columbia. It has its own 'hausmountain', in this case dramatic Mount Hood, 11,239 feet, always snow-covered and an excellent site for experienced skiers, many of whom are helicoptered to the summit for a tremendous descent. The next big mountain in the Cascades up from Hood is the less kindly Mount St Helens which erupted so violently in 1980.

The back country of Oregon is almost as wild as it was in the days when settlers came over the famous Trail to The Dalles on the Columbia River and then floated down to found Portland. A railway, served by a train of AMTRAK suitably named "The Pioneer", runs up beside the river, and then strikes through wilderness to cross the Pemberton Mountains. It goes through Boise, Idaho's small capital, and eventually reaches Ogden and Salt Lake City in Utah.

They call mountainous Idaho the 'Gem State' but it refers to gems of scenic beauty, not the mineral kind. This is a big State, like all the Western ones, extending to 83,557 square miles, with a short border shared with British Columbia in the North. Less than 900,000 people live in it, so there is a great deal of wilderness.

Idaho can boast the deepest gorge in the nation, Hells Canyon, which the dare-devil motorcyclist Evil Kanevil tried without success to leap across. It has the fast flowing Salmon River down which intrepid rafters ride, and it has the Craters of the Moon National Park. It became well known for its Sun Valley ski resort, developed by the Union Pacific Railroad in time for the Winter Olympics of 1932, where Sogne Henjie of Norway did so well.

The capital city, Boise, in the southwestern section of Idaho, has boomed in recent years to reach a population of 95,000, by far the largest in the State. There are three domes on the capitol building, the central one rearing to 210 feet and made of white marble. The city was first settled in 1850 but remained insignificant until Idaho became a State in 1890.

A favourite small town of mine is Bonner's Ferry, on the route of AMTRAK's "Empire Builder" where it crosses the Kootenai River. Close to the Canadian border, it is where Chief Joseph and his Nez Perce Indian warriors fought and lost after a 1300 mile chase in 1877.

This great inland empire of Oregon and Idaho is for back-packers and people wanting to get away from it all. Nicknamed the Beaver State, Oregon is 97,000 square miles – twice the size of England with Wales – but has a population of less than 2½ millions. About a fifth of the people live in Greater Portland.

But go South from Portland by road along US 101 and in fine weather one will discover some of the most magnificent coastal scenery in the world. Highway 101 clings to the dramatic coast for several hundred miles, down to the California border and far beyond. The massive continental USA collides, as it were, with the Pacific Ocean in a series of cliffs and headlands. No matter how light the wind is, the foam from the Pacific breakers swirls into an eerie mist around oddly shaped rocks. The beaches are littered with driftwood and the tang in the air is surely a reminder of the finest ozone.

I came upon a delightful village beside the sea, facing a sandy beach flanked by giant rocks. It was called Port

Orford, and in the Port Orford Motel (there was another one but less attractive) I spent one of the best nights I have ever known in the United States. It was comfortable, warm, and cheap. So was the cafe next door, which excelled itself with big portions of well cooked food at prices which were low even by Oregon standards. This State does not apply Sales Tax, and its cost of living is one of the lowest in the country, prices for food, transport, accommodation, and general goods making British, French and German eyebrows lift in amazement.

Further South there is a deep indentation called Coos Bay, the only harbour apart from the mouth of the Columbia far to the North. The road goes around this not very attractive place and heads for the California border. It will have shown the traveller the very best of the Oregon coastline, while a trip inland to the East of Portland will have shown its gorges and wild mountains which are at least the equal of the splendour of neighbouring Washington State.

12.   States of Contrast

Alaska & Hawaii

Background

Admitted to the Union in 1959 as the 49th and 50th States, Alaska and Hawaii have little in common apart from not being part of the mainland USA. Indeed they are States of contrast, the furthest North and the furthest South, the coldest and the warmest, the largest and the third smallest, one was purchased (from the Russians), the other was annexed.

However, both the 'new' States (and new is a reasonable description since the 48th State – Arizona – was admitted 47 years earlier) share the waters of the Pacific Ocean, the same Humpback whales, and active volcanoes connected by the Rim of Fire.

Alaska, now well established on the tourist map, is still a wild frontier State with less than one person per square mile. It might well have been part of the contiguous United States if an early movement among pioneers entering the Pacific North West had succeeded with their expedition to drive the British North Americans up to latitude 54 degrees 50 minutes. They would then have had a common border with the Russians who owned Alaska. The volunteers, who did not have the backing of the American Government in Washington, advanced under the slogan "Fifty four fifty or fight". The only casualty of the skirmishes was a cow, but if the invaders of British Columbia had reached their determined latitude, there would have been no city of Vancouver. As it was the border remained along the 49th parallel, although this is varied slightly on the Pacific Coast to take account of islands and inlets.

Alaska

Alaska begins as a thin coastal strip quite far to the South, so much so that the small city of Ketchikan is below Edinburgh on a line traced across the globe. A warm current keeps all of this coast ice-free and relatively temperate, like that of the Norwegian coastline. Next to the Caribbean, it has become the most cruised region in the world, with a vast fleet of competing ships sailing through the islands and up the inlets between May and September.

It is the big hunk of Alaska stretching to the Arctic Ocean which is the wilderness, where winter lasts for nine months of the year. Oil exploration has made an impact upon it, and an oil pipeline runs down from the frigid 'North Slope' to the ice-free waters at Valdez over a distance of 789 miles. The metal tube was controversial in 1973 when the Pipeline Bill was signed, and it remains so, environmentalists constantly challenging it for its theoretical effect upon wildlife.

I have stood on a specially built viewing platform on a fine July day on the opposite side of the inlet to Valdez, and seen the pipeline snaking over the Chugach Mountains and down to the oil terminal. It is an amazing piece of work, rapidly completed, and has not had the feared effect of wildlife, although, ironically, these waters have been sadly polluted by a Tanker spill due to a navigation error. Incidentally, oil takes just over three days to flow from the frozen North Slope to the terminal, moving through the pipeline at about 11 miles per hour.

Oil has brought tremendous wealth to Alaska, worth several thousand dollars to every inhabitant every year. The Gold Rush on the Klondyke which was in Canada's Yukon Territory, brought only a trickle, mainly from supply work and transport, but back in 1898 it did much to put Alaska on the map.

After purchase from the Russians in 1867 the vast territory lay largely undisturbed for three decades. Things Russian slowly became things American, but right now the vogue is to emphasise the Russian history. Hotels and streets bear the names of Russian governors and merchants; Russian artefacts are in great demand. But the Russians did little with their massive land beyond fishing the coasts and settling the gentler islands.

Alaska is not just the largest State of America, it is more than twice the size of Texas, the next largest. It would happily envelope Britain, France, Spain and Portugal, and leave room for the Netherlands and Denmark! There are very few roads, but air transport is well developed, especially with small planes landing on skis. There is an extremely good ferry system, while a Government Railroad links Seward and Whittaker with Anchorage and up through the wilderness to Fairbanks.

The daily train "Aurora" is the best way to see the inland, or if one can afford it, from the great vista domes of a private de luxe train which in summer follows up the "Aurora". The route passes close to America's highest mountain, McKinley, 20,320 feet, which rears above the recently named Denali National Park. In fact the schedule in each direction allows for a daylight journey of some 11 hours for the 356 miles from Anchorage to Fairbanks. The seaport of Whittier is 63 miles southeast of Anchorage, served by a separate shuttle train.

An amazing system called Alaskan State Maritime Highway means competent Government ferries having the same status as major roads down in the mainland USA. This is the inexpensive way to go to Alaska, starting formerly at Seattle and now from a port specially built for cars and rolling freight north of that city. An express ferry takes three days to reach Juneau, Alaska's capital.

The terminal in Alaska for the big ferries is Skagway, the most historic and most visited town in the State. But on the way from Juneau they call at Haines, where a road goes to join the Alcan Highway and allows a drive to Anchorage. There is still no physical way apart from flying to get from the State capital to Anchorage, the largest city. Travellers must use a ferry and then a bus, or take cars with them on the ships, driving them from Haines except in mid-winter.

All of the endless procession of cruise ships call at Skagway and until rationing was introduced recently, they all entered Glacier Bay, fantastic home of calving ice bergs and numerous glaciers curving down to the waters. Some ships go on across the Gulf of Alaska to the mighty

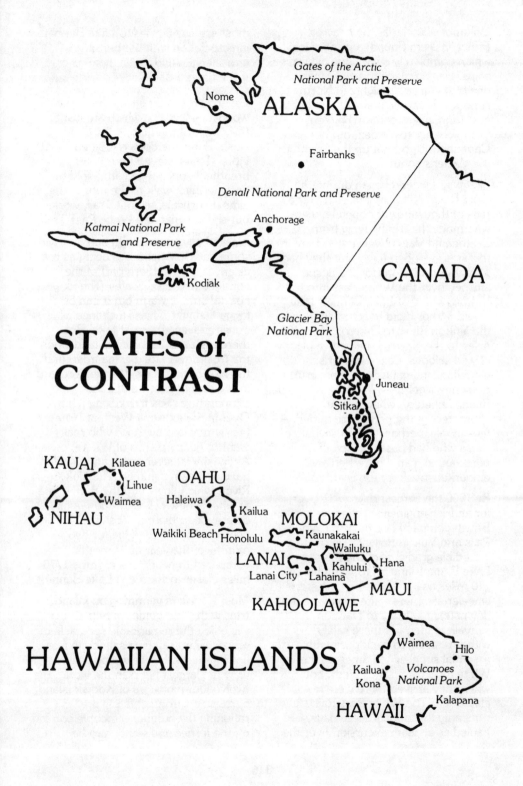

STATES of CONTRAST

ALASKA

Gates of the Arctic
National Park and Preserve

Nome

Fairbanks

Denali National Park and Preserve

Anchorage

Katmai National Park
and Preserve

Kodiak

CANADA

Glacier Bay
National Park

Juneau

Sitka

KAUAI Kilauea
Lihue
Waimea

OAHU
Haleiwa
Kailua

NIHAU

Waikiki Beach Honolulu

MOLOKAI
Kaunakakai

Wailuku

LANAI
Lanai City Lahaina

Kahului Hana

KAHOOLAWE

MAUI

HAWAIIAN ISLANDS

Waimea Hilo
Kailua Volcanoes
Kona National Park
Kalapana

HAWAII

Columbia Glacier at the head of Prince William Sound, a giant of ice which completely dwarfs the big cruise ships. Having made this trip I feel it is one of the greatest sights in North America. It can be made at much less cost (and in less comfort) by ferry from Whittier to Valdez, but not all Captains will go right up the Sound to the glacier's snout.

Skagway's legend began during the Gold Rush, receiving the bulk of the tens of thousands of hopeful miners who made the trip by ferry from Seattle and Vancouver. It was here in this small wooden town that they had to gather provisions for the desperate journey over the White Pass into the Yukon, where at Lake Bennett they would find or build boats to float down the Yukon River to Dawson City, 400 miles to the North. It became a place of wild saloons, dance hall girls, gambling, and gangsters. Most cruise passengers get to walk up to the Gold Rush Cemetery, where many characters of the period are buried. A few people, perhaps one in seventy of those who had passed through northbound, came back rich and embarked in a ferry for Seattle.

By 1900 the fiercest days were over, for an Irish engineer backed by a British company had built the White Pass and Yukon Railway, up over the incredible gradients of the Pass to Lake Bennett and on to Whitehorse, 110 miles away, where big safe stern-wheeler steamers waited to make the downsteam journey to Dawson. Travellers then got there safely, without having to back-pack with essential supplies ten times up the White Pass (thousands died), but when they arrived there were few claims left. The White Pass Railway runs only for tourists these days, hauled as a steam excursion over the most scenic 40 miles to Lake Bennett in association with the berthing of cruise ships (and that can be up to three times a day).

On any visit to Skagway, tread the wooden sidewalks, which are just as they were at the time of the Gold Rush. Enter the domed Golden North Hotel (I have stayed there) and breathe its unchanged atmosphere. If time permits, walk to the foot of the almost vertical Chilkoot Trail, worse but shorter than the White Pass Trail.

Alaska has a short bright summer with some days in Anchorage being as hot as any in the northern part of the contiguous United States. The long coastal strip is warm but it can be foggy and wet. This is a chance all cruise passengers must take. But there are parts of the giant land where the frost never lifts (perma-frost) and the North Slope oil settlements regard it as a sort of heat wave if the temperature rises to freezing point. Over in the extreme West, at Nome (easily reached by those who really want to go, by planes of Wien Alaska Airlines) it is never warm and usually hazy or wet in summer. The Yukon River, which flows into the Bering Sea at what is now called Emmonak in deference to the Inuit (Eskimo) people, is only free of ice for two months of the year at its mouth, compared to nearly five months 1770 miles closer to source at Lake Bennett.

Most travellers venturing on inland trips with good guides in September will enjoy the remarkable spectacle of grizzly bears catching salmon in fast flowing rivers. Fewer will be able to view the largest bears in the world, the twelve foot monsters of Kodiak Island, because environmentalists are rationing the number of people coming off the ferries and wanting to be escorted through the National Wild Life Refuge at the southwestern end of the big island.

Alaska's largest creatures are shared with Hawaii, the Humpback whales which disport in the icy waters of Glacier Bay in summer, where the plankton are plentiful. Again, limiting the number of ships entering this long fragile inlet stops many people from seeing the mammals. However, they all set off for the warm waters of Maui in the State of Hawaii and there the whale watching is unrestricted as they crash around the Pacific between Lanai and the old whaling town of Lahaina on Maui. Here they breed and later take their young back to Glacier Bay around Maytime.

Hawaii
The State of Hawaii, admitted to the Union on August 21, 1959, consists of eight main islands, only six of which can be visited. The six are the 'big island' of Hawaii, Maui, Lanai, Molokai, Oahu, and Kauai. Kahoolawe is entirely used by US military and naval forces, mainly as a target area, while Niihai is privately owned and tightly closed, one object being to try to keep pure blooded Polynesian Hawaiians from mixing with the polyglot inhabitants of the other islands.

Honolulu is the capital, situated on Oahu, close to the famous Waikiki Beach and sheltered by equally famous Diamond Head. It embraces Pearl Harbor which sprang into dramatic prominence on December 6, 1941, with the Japanese surprise attack. Pearl Harbor is a memorial, and curiously enough gets almost as many Japanese visitors paying respects as it does Americans.

More than one million people a year file through the serene memorial built on the upturned hull of the battleship USS "Arizona", the worst casualty of the bombing which destroyed a large portion of the United States Pacific Fleet.

Only two big hotels stood on Waikiki Beach when I first saw it, and at that time the best Beach views and access was from the US Army base. It was easy to walk the Beach from end to end. But now there are so many major hotels that they stand cheek-by-jowl, all with what they claim to be 'private beaches on Waikiki' but in fact that only applies above the high water mark.

This is an exhilarating place, especially at night, when Kalakua Avenue, running on the landward side of the hotels, is busy and brilliantly lit. But some of the tropical delight of Oahu has been lost along the way, at its best probably in the days of Matson Line, once – with its luxury liners – the only link to the American mainland. Matson, in fact, owned the two hotels, the Royal Hawaiian (known as the 'Pink Palace' where they still float an orchid in your cocktail) built for first class passengers, and the lesser but still attractive Moana Hotel, aimed mostly at the tourist class passengers. They are both well over sixty years old, while between them and on either side are giants constructed within the past 15 years.

One good thing for today's visitors is the clear, unobstructed view of Diamond Head. Tobacco heiress Doris Duke had built a massive luxury apartment block on the side of the dramatic headland, and this blot on the viewscape stayed for nearly 20 years before being removed.

Surf runs in on Waikiki and surf boards are seen in plenty but it is gentle stuff. To see the mighty

117

breakers which are 'ridden' by the experts it is necessary to go to Makaha Beach on the West side of Oahu, and here thirty footers come crashing in with surfers sweeping ashore (or getting wiped out) at high speed.

It is extremely easy and cheap to get around Oahu thanks to an excellent air-conditioned bus service going right round the island at less than $2. Even where changes have to be made, a free transfer is available. This works out at one of the cheapest and longest scenic bus rides in the world; it shows passengers such sights as Waimea Bay, Crouching Lion Rock dominating Kahana Bay, Koko Head, and the Halana Blowhole.

The main international airport is close to Honolulu, where flights from the mainland arrive with great frequency. It is the departure point for inter-island flights by three companies. The only other airport with direct flights to mainland America is on the Big Island at Hilo on the Northwestern coast. There is a 'common fare' allowing passengers to ride cheaply to each island once if they hold a roundtrip ticket from mainland America.

Travel between the islands is disappointingly poor. Long gone are the days of the Matson inter-island steamers, and now it is impossible to find a ferry to take a car and driver. Cars can be sent, in flat barges towed by tugs, but passengers (and the driver) must fly, which adds greatly to the cost. Each island has relatively cheap car hire systems at the airports, but the whole scheme needs bringing up-to-date, with suitable car ferries. Boeing jetfoils have failed on the inter-island routes (they did not carry cars anyway) due to heavy Pacific swells. A new semi-submersible scheme has not been launched successfully despite much preparation.

The best way by far to see the islands is to take a cruise in two big ships, both American flag liners, "Independence" and "Constitution", 20,000 tons, with two raked funnels and counter sterns. They are coming up to 40 years old but graceful and comfortable, operating from Honolulu back to Honolulu each week, giving seven nights. They run to different itineraries but ensure landing on all open islands except Molokai. This, however, is a fairly costly inclusive cruise and sections cannot be made.

The Big Island of Hawaii has the fierce active volcanoes, Mauna Loa, 13,680 feet, and Mauna Kea, 13,796 feet (the highest peak in the Pacific). Their vast lava fields of black rock and the black beaches from the outflow are unique, now formed into a National Park. Kilauea, only 4,700 feet, is much more active than the two bigger ones, and is frequently seen erupting with a curious thin liquid lava locally called 'a-a' which spurts high to make vivid colours at night. Near these volcanoes it is dangerous terrain and one must enquire locally if it is safe to drive or walk in the vicinity.

There is one other danger in Hawaii, particularly affecting the Big Island. It is the Tsunami, or Pacific Tidal Wave. These days observatories give adequate warning, but in the past appalling damage and loss of life has occurred. There used to be a railway system on the Big Island, but a giant Tsunami swept ashore and roared through the lowlands, overwhelming a train and all its passengers. The name is Japanese, the waves having been noted close to the shores of Nippon arising from undersea eruptions.

The island of Hawaii boasts the most

southerly point in the United States, Ka Lae (South Cape), prodding below 19 degrees of latitude and thus at least 250 miles into the Tropics. All the inhabited islands are below the Tropic of Cancer, sharing a warm to hot climate, very wet at times (Mount Waialeale on Kauai is one of the rainiest spots in the world). Best is Trade Wind-cooled November to March.

Everybody who goes there loves Maui, variously called the 'Honeymoon Island', and the 'House of the Sun Island'. On its western shore, looking towards the pineapple island of Lanai, is a cluster of some of the finest resort hotels in the world, including a Sheraton, a Hyatt and a Marriott. These are between Kaanapali and Lahaina, a five mile stretch. Worth riding is a steam railway restored from an old sugar line, which provides a colourful journey through plantations – the Lahaina, Kaanapali and Pacific Railroad. Trains are met by old London buses which feed passengers to the hotels or to the shops in Lahaina.

Haleakala, which actually does mean 'House of the Sun', is a magnificent National Park in a gigantic amphitheatre below Red Hill rearing to 10,000 feet. There is a Lodge where hardy folk get up early to enjoy the spectacular sunrise and climb to the extinct volcanic craters.

Captain James Cook found the islands, which he called the Sandwich Group. He came ashore at Waimea on Kauai in 1778 and was treated as a god at first, though he was murdered later when some local stuck a spear in him and he groaned – immortals should not feel pain! Because of Cook, the Hawaiian State flag still has a Union Jack embodied in it. Kings and Queens make up the history of the Hawaiian Islands after Cook and some monarchs, notably King Kamehameha III and Queen Lilioukalani. The latter was deposed in 1894, when the islands became a Republic headed by the American Sanford Dole, whose descendants are still closely involved with the pineapple business on Lanai. But in 1898, the United States annexed the islands.

American conscience is probably the root cause of the great tendency to romanticise the past royalty of Hawaii. There are Royal Balls, and other 'Royal' occasions, with 'Royal' palaces to visit and 'Royal' legends to hear. The names of dead monarchs from the past crop up everywhere.

Kauai has a wild shoreline, some parts steep and inaccessible but its claim to scenic fame is the 'Grand Canyon of the Pacific', Waimea Canyon, a massive rent in the earth which can be viewed from suitable overlooks. Its depth is 3,600 feet and its length ten miles; the quiet is amazing, often the only sounds being the flapping of strange birds' wings.

I said earlier that Waialeale is among the wettest places in the world. It gets an average of 480 inches a year. But do not be put off by this threat of rain – the leeward side of the island, where most hotels are, has almost desert conditions (for the Tropics) with a mere 15 to 20 inches.

13. Travel Tips and Information

Air

There are significant travel bargains for any visitors coming to the United States from more than a thousand miles beyond the country's borders. They apply to airlines, the railway system, and the Greyhound bus network on the basis of 'go-as-you-please' tickets valid from one week to one month. However, they must be purchased outside the United States.

Some airlines offer special tickets in connection with their own trans-Atlantic fares which appear to give an edge over their competition. But in the main, all qualifying travellers can buy in advance the various air bargains, which may permit four flight sectors for as low as fifty Dollars each, or a system-wide ticket valid for up to three weeks. The small print on these must always be carefully studied for they are complicated and can be quite restrictive, such as not allowing the passenger to transit the same city twice or having to pay a supplement on certain Friday and Sunday flights.

Flying is not, of course, the best way to see the United States but in such a large country it is obviously the quickest way to travel distances of more than 300 miles. The go-as-you-please tickets are ideal for people who have in mind visiting a few cities to meet up with friends or relatives in a short space of time, or to see specific areas coupled with a rental car from destination airports. Frequent visitors to America who have already seen a good deal of what lies below may also find these air tickets an excellent way of covering a large area.

Bus

Greyhound buses were the first to offer a nation-wide bargain ticket, beginning in 1961 under the first 'Visit America' campaign when they sold '99 days for 99 Dollars'. This offer was extremely popular with students from all over the world, who often slept aboard the buses on their long journeys. The competing Trailways system now merged with Greyhound soon followed suit but never achieved the fame and success of Greyhound. Both systems are rather fragmented these days, and a severe strike 6 months long in 1990 has resulted in a decline in service. Greyhound still has visitor tickets which cover the whole country, called Ameripass and selling overseas in currencies relative to the country of purchase. For Britons buying them in Britain in 1990 they are seven days for £85, 15 days for £135, and 30 days for £170, and for Germans buying in Germany (Frankfurt is European Head Office of Greyhound) the prices are 240 Deutsche Marks, 390, and 500 respectively. These tickets are valid for East and West Canada as well, but *not* trans-continental in that country. A new fourday Ameripass is on the market costing £45 sterling (115 DM's).

Holders of the go-as-you-please

Ameripass simply tear off a coupon from the book written to their own route requirements, then present it to an agent at the terminal or way-station. Greyhound has no reservation system (this saves the organisation countless millions of Dollars annually). Instead, the bus line guarantees a ride for anyone turning up at a Greyhound depot with a valid ticket. If the scheduled bus is full they will run a second one, or in the case of perhaps one or two passengers beyond capacity, will charter a taxi to follow the bus. This happened to me in Oregon, the taxi behind the scheduled San Francisco bus all the way to Klamath Falls, near the California border, where I was able to take up vacated seats with my companion. This cost nothing, and as for Greyhound, they accept the charge as only a fraction of what computerised booking systems would cost.

Greyhound and Trailways where still fully in action have their terminals and depots as near to the heart of a town or city as possible, and provide food counters with basic quick-service hot dishes (not always appetising) for sale. Baggage is checked free and loaded by the agent. Drivers, many of whom own shares in the Corporation, never speak to passengers when the bus is in motion. Smoking is limited to the last three rows of seats and only then if the State permits it (Oregon, for example, does not). All buses are air conditioned, with slightly reclining seats, and there is a small washroom at the end of each vehicle.

Going by bus is the cheapest way to travel, but much of the riding is on Inter-State highways which do not always show off the best scenery. High average speeds are maintained with a steady maximum of 60 to 65 miles an hour where the law permits (for 13

years the US-wide maximum was 55 and this is still enforced by some states). Between some cities up to 150 miles apart, Greyhound and Trailways buses are the fastest means of transport, on a centre to centre basis, particularly so between Seattle and Vancouver, British Columbia, where there is now no train service and getting to and from airports takes a great deal of time. All kinds of people ride the buses, even on some short sectors those in business, but mainly the average age tends to be high and the riders aiming at economy.

Rail

Rail travel in the United States is in the hands of a semi-Government organisation called AMTRAK, a Federal Corporation launched in April 1971 to take over passenger operations from a large number of private railroads, including some affected by bankruptcy. It is a skeleton service but the bones are good.

On a long distance basis, trains tend to run once a day, while in busy corridors such as Washington to New York, New York to Boston, and New York to Albany, services are fast and frequent. Los Angeles to San Diego is also fast and frequent while Chicago to Detroit has not yet been developed beyond three rather slow trains a day, and from New York to Florida three fast services plus an 'Auto-train' carrying passengers with their cars.

Some of the once-a-day long haul trains are equal to the best in the world, great named services such as "Empire Builder" (Chicago to Seattle and Portland), "California Zephyr" (Chicago to San Francisco via Denver and Salt Lake City), "South West Chief" (Chicago to Los Angeles via Kansas City and Albuquerque), and "Coast Daylight/Starlight" (Seattle to

Los Angeles via Sacramento) offering high standards of comfort and recreational facilities. Three times a week services, the "Eagle" (Chicago to Texas) and "Sunset Limited" (New Orleans to Los Angeles via Houston) are equally well equipped.

It is not cheap to ride a good train and if using a sleeping car (the best on Superliner equipment having private showers) the cost may exceed first class by air. But meals are included for sleeper passengers and facilities for rest and relaxation are unsurpassed. There is space to move, read, eat, sleep, and watch the scenery from a high level glass-roofed car with swivel armchairs (also available to non-sleeper 'coach class' passengers).

AMTRAK issues regional and nation-wide go-as-you-please tickets called USARAILPASS, sold in the United States, but overseas at half rate. The 1990 prices are, in Dollars, nationwide 299, Eastern Region (East Coast to the Mississippi including Chicago and New Orleans) 179, Western Region (from the Mississippi to all points West) 229, Far Western (excludes middle America and trans-continental) 179, and Florida 59. All passes are valid for 45 days. Slight increases are forecast for 1991.

These passes must be purchased overseas at AMTRAK agencies. Britons are the largest users of them followed by Germans and Australians. They are good for 'coach' travel but may be upgraded to sleeper on payment of the relevant fare (this can be quite stiff for the best accommodation) and upgraded to high speed Metroliner travel between New York and Washington. Using the passes works in a similar way to the bus system, whereby a passenger presents it, plus a Passport, to a ticket agent for the route ticket to be prepared. There is one snag. Many long distance trains are fully booked months in advance and most trains require reservations (free). This can limit chance travel plans.

Car Hire/Rental

Car rental throughout the United States is intensely used, with big and small companies in the business having desks at airports, major railroad stations, and in downtown locations. There is more car renting in the nation than in the rest of the world put together, for Americans cannot bear to be without 'wheels'. Competition among companies is fierce and many special rates are offered. Avis, Hertz, National, Budget and Dollar are paramount among those providing reductions for foreign visitors booking cars in advance, mainly from gateway airports.

It is much cheaper to hire a car in USA than almost anywhere else in the world. Even so, rates vary widely, Florida being the cheapest, only half those charged in New York and New England. Collision Damage Waiver adds a good deal to the daily or weekly rate, but is essential if a big bill for a slight knock is to be avoided. Hirers should check that the write-off and injury insurance is sufficient in the light of high medical charges; it may be desirable to 'top up'. State taxes will be added to the rental charge, except in those few states not applying it. Almost invariably, one thousand free miles are allowed on a week's rental.

Thanks to a generally excellent standard of driving and a good highway system, well sign posted and patrolled, no driver from overseas should feel that renting a car and driving around – even in cities – will be complicated or dangerous. In some cities, or even Western towns, where the sprawl is getting worse and

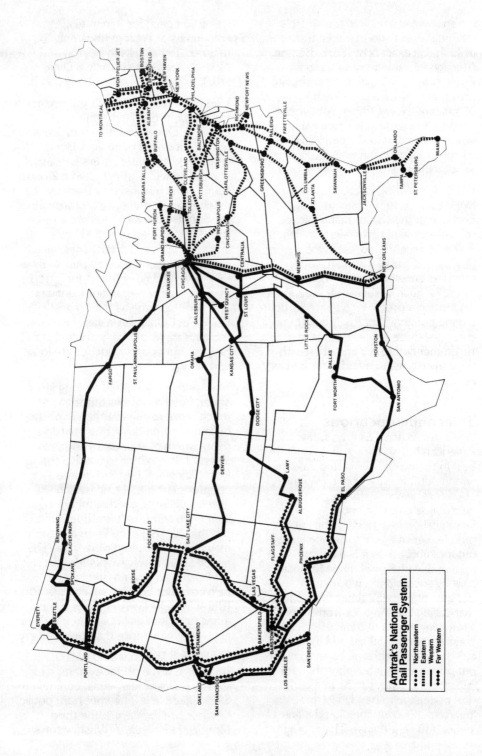

Amtrak's National
Rail Passenger System

●●●● Northeastern
●●●●●● Eastern
—— Western
◆◆◆◆ Far Western

distances alarming, car transport is essential. Really good public transport in such places as New York, Boston, Chicago, Washington, D.C., San Francisco, Los Angeles, Sacramento, the cities of the Pacific North West, Miami, and New Orleans, obviates the need to hire a car. Otherwise the visitor without 'wheels' can be like a visitor to a European city getting about without shoes!

While signposting is good on major highways it is sometimes at short notice with the risk of being 'picked off' unless maintaining alert driving. It is always essential to know the direction of travel with highway numbers showing 'West', 'East' etc. There is much verbiage on road signs presenting a problem to those without a good command of English. Where there are three or more lanes it is recommended to try and stick with the centre ones to avoid a compulsory, sudden, exit.

Telecommunications

While not as good as it was, the American telephone system is still the best in the world. Misrouted calls and wrong numbers are very rare, while operators answer with courtesy, helpfulness and efficiency. Deregulation has made some calls more expensive by shortening limits, but for subscribers it is a cheap system. No charge is made for local calls by subscribers, while long distance at off-peak times is so cheap that calling Los Angeles from New York can mean a two minute conversation for 50 cents! Ubiquitous call boxes or booths all seem to work but prices are much higher than for subscribers. It pays to have a good deal of change to hand, say three 'quarters' (25 cent coins) and a few 'dimes' (10 cent coins). The average

call is 25 cents, for 4 minutes, sometimes at peak periods only 3 minutes. Local calls in Boston and New Orleans are still only a Dime (10c).

Like mailing services everywhere in the world, the United States Post Office (a Government institution) is not as good as it once was. But it works and for basic letters is relatively cheap and fast. Letters need a 25 cent stamp, which transports them by rail on shorter journeys, by air throughout the country. One can expect a next day delivery even for a 3000 mile internal mailing. But packages, which escalate in cost ounce by ounce, may take several days. Stamps for letters overseas are 50 cents but Canada is charged the same as the domestic USA. Post Offices are easily recognised, flying the Stars and Stripes, but counter queues are long and slow.

Stamps may be bought at drug stores and in hotel machines but they are much more expensive than in postal buildings, often delivering only 35 cents worth of stamps for 50 cents inserted. It is better to make a trip to a Post Office and buy, either at a counter or at a machine (which will give full value) a good number of stamps to last for a visit. It is vital to put the ZIP (Area) code on a letter; it may not be delivered otherwise. The postal service only works Mondays to Fridays; there are no Saturday deliveries nor Sunday collections. RFD (Rural Free Delivery) may in some areas have just one collection; no one anywhere gets more than one delivery.

Public Holidays mean no postal services but the phone system, and Western Union telegrams, continue to work effectively. The important public holidays are January 1, the third Monday in February (Washington's

Birthday), Good Friday, the last Monday in May (Memorial Day), July 4 (Independence Day), the first Monday in September (Labor Day), second Monday in October (Columbus Day), November 11 (Armistice Day or Veterans Day), the fourth Thursday in November (Thanksgiving Day), December 25. Only Independence Day, Thanksgiving Day, and Christmas Day close all stores and bring many functions to a halt. There are Jewish holidays or festivals which severely cripple business in New York, especially Rosh Hashana (Jewish New Year), in September.

Medical

It is recognised that American hospitals and medical facilities in general are outstanding, but they are extremely expensive. Although many Americans are members of Blue Cross or have medical welfare, there is no equivalent to free treatment or a National Health service. In their best interests, visitors must take out health insurance before arriving in the United States. This must cover up to one million dollars (bills have been known to exceed that sum for heart attacks, intensive care and lengthy treatment). Even two days in hospital with nursing and a minor operation can easily cost seven thousand Dollars. A policy valid for three weeks can be obtained from most insurers for about £35, in England, to 100 DM's in Germany.

Tipping

America is the land of the tip, a custom going back in history and an essential smoothing of one's path in city life. Taxi drivers expect 15 percent and if they do not get it, show contempt in several ways, not least by their squeal of tyres as they drive away. In hotels, (not motels) the

baggage handler gets a Dollar, more if the bags are heavy. It is usual to leave the chambermaid an envelope with two Dollars if staying a couple of nights, five Dollars for a week, even is she is unseen during the stay. Airlines do not expect tips but a 'Skycap' expects one or two Dollars if helping with baggage. If using a sleeping car on a train, an overnight two Dollars to the porter is customary if he is helpful.

Customs

Entering the country means encountering formalities at airports, shipping piers, and land frontiers. A visa is no longer essential for Britons if they are purely on holiday and are in possession of a round trip ticket but they are still advisable. Visas are issued by US Embassies at their consulate sections, and are free but it may take three weeks to obtain one. The usual type allows multiple entry and lasts indefinitely, at least for the life of the Passport. Visas for study and work require a great deal of formality.

On entry a visitor receives an ID 94 form marking the period of the stay. This must be kept in the Passport and returned on departure from the country. Some airports have long lines at the immigration booths and it can take 90 minutes to clear the officials. At remote land frontiers it is quick and easy and the solitary official may even offer a cup of coffee while he or she completes the ID 94 form.

Customs everywhere are strict, mainly searching for drugs. There are red and green channels at some busy airports but passengers must make an oral declaration and be given a clearance form. Every person entering the United States must complete a brief written customs declaration, even if writing 'nil', and it must be signed. On aircraft, flight staff will issue the immigration and customs forms well before landing. If carrying cash, only 5000 Dollars or more needs declaring.

The importation of fresh fruit is totally prohibited, and some states prohibit it as well, California in particular, on inter state journeys.

Electrics
Despite the growth of tourism, American electrical fittings remain insular, and it is essential to have the right plug to fit into a wall socket. This will be for 110 Volts throughout the country. It is wise to carry a travellers plug (which covers the American two-prong) and an adaptor.

14.   Costs, Eating Out and Drink, Shopping

Costs

Because the United States is composed of 50 different states all with their own laws, owing allegiance to the Federal system in Washington, costs and taxes must vary widely. Many geographical considerations enter into the picture, and so does transportation.

Even in a small country like Belgium, the cost of living will vary between the Flemish coastal areas and the Walloon uplands. In Britain, geographical factors make costs in far flung islands (Shetlands, Isles of Scilly, and the Outer Hebrides) higher than in densely populated parts of mainland England. But in the United States, aided by tax variations, costs are quite dramatically different.

Probably the only fixed charge that people in Mississippi share with those in New York State or California is the Federal income tax. Virtually everything else will be different, from a can of beans to a gallon of gasolene, from sales tax to a packet of cigarettes. Each State has its own cost of living, and no two are the same. There is an annual Consumer Price Index issued by Washington, D.C., but that is more the concern of people living, working and spending (also paying taxes) in their various regions.

What is of more concern to the visitor from abroad is a figure worked out by Federal officials showing the cost of three meals in a day, accommodation in a first class hotel for one night,

public transport fares, two taxi rides, a modest amount of drink, and a packet of cigarettes. In Washington this is taken as the base level of 100. The rating for New York City is 116, for Boston 112, for San Francisco 88, Atlanta (Georgia) 67, Raleigh (North Carolina) 56, and Austin, Texas, only 47. These figures can change almost month by month but they do serve as some guide (they were 1988 assessments) to the costs a tourist might encounter. Alaska is by far the most expensive (Anchorage 151).

Tourists are not excused Sales Tax, a levy applied in most States to everything purchased including food. But the States of Oregon and New Hampshire do not have Sales Tax, which appears to make purchases cheaper, and can save up to ten Dollars on the cost of hotel rooms. But other items might be more pricey than in States with a Sales Tax, for example a pack of 20 cigarettes being $1.30 in New Hampshire but only 70 cents (plus Sales Tax of 5 cents) in North Carolina.

The United States are in general cheaper than Britain, Germany, France, Switzerland, Italy, Austria and Scandinavia. This has been so for twenty years. In pre-war days, America was cheaper than in Britain (and that was cheap enough) with 4.83 Dollars to the Pound. From 1940 to 1970 it was more expensive. Today, despite only about 1.90 to the Pound, it is cheaper, and infinitely cheaper than

Germany. So much so in the latter case that many common items, from a cup of coffee to a tax ride, are three times more costly in Germany. Travelling with a former German Naval Officer in Alabama, we ordered a bowl of giant shrimps. They came with a dish of peanuts. "How much?" asked my companion. "95 cents" said the waiter. "Yes, vor ze Peanuts, but how much for ze Prawns?" The waiter looked amazed. "We give you the peanuts with the shrimps".

Inflation is the factor in all cost comparisons. There is steady inflation throughout USA but it has been at a lower rate than in Europe. Especially when costs escalated in the early 1970s. Typical price rises show gasolene up from a 1972 figure of 34 cents a gallon in California to $1.25 today, New York subway fares up from 35 cents to $1.25, a good motel room in Texas up from 9 Dollars (for two people) to 25 Dollars today.

Items which continue to be significantly more costly than in Britain include any kind of chocolate, any kind of drug, and medical care. The latter is beyond reason and all visitors *must* be insured, even to a million Dollars, to take care of any medical emergency. Imported alcoholic drinks are more expensive than in Europe, and good domestic wines are by no means cheap. Real marmalade is costly to the point of absurdity (most Americans use locally made jellies at breakfast); visitors should take a pot of the real thing. In fact, marmalade gets the same kind of 'hype' as other imported items such as Gucci products, Dom Perignon Champagne, and Mercedes cars!

It is reasonable to say that everything else, especially food, is cheaper than in Britain or Western Europe. Unless

patronising some exclusive boutique (there are many of these in Beverly Hills), clothing and especially mens' shirts and womens' shoes, are inexpensive.

Eating out

The range of places to eat is fantastic. There is no inhabited spot, however small, that does not have at least two 'eateries'. Restaurants come at all levels, with several thousand easily recognised MacDonalds, Burger Kings, Kentucky Fried Chicken, and Dairy Queens, usually on the long strips outside towns and cities. These serve fast foods, not necessarily 'junk foods' which one hears a lot about, and they are cheap and quick.

A rank above the 'fast foods' are the 'short order' restaurants, always found on strips and sometimes in cities, with the excellent provision of parking lots for customers. The best of these, in my opinion, based upon years of using them, are the International House of Pancakes chain, conspicuous by their bright blue, often steepled, roofs, and Shoneys (where any senior citizen gets at least a Dollar off the check).

There is full waitress service, and a large menu, while breakfasts are superb with six bottles of syrups of various kinds for pancakes. One is not, of course, obliged to order pancakes; simply that they specialise in them, sometimes meat-filled, sometimes jam or ice cream stuffed. Denny's is another of the short order type, while different regions have others. They are open 24 hours a day, with shifts.

Diners, a great American custom, the premises shaped like a pre-war dining car on the railroads, are still to be found but tend to be dwindling. This is counter service with orders carried out in time-honoured fashion by shouting to the cook in almost unintelligible words. Prices are between the fast food and short order places. They may not always be open.

Most smaller cities and towns have one or two family-run restaurants with names like "Mother MacMarnies". This can mean American home cooking at its best, but not always. If driving, the way to check is to see that there are plenty of cars parked outside and that there is plenty of light in the cafe. In general, prices will be slightly above the short order places but still modest. Some, of course, will be Italian or Greek.

At the general level, American meals are good value and nearly always pleasant to eat. Risks begin at the higher levels, when 'gourmet food' is advertised, and the tables are lit only by dim electric candles. The more they pretend to be gourmet the less likelihood of a good value meal, and prices are often higher the darker they are. In almost all city guides there are restaurant listings but they pay for inclusion. Obviously there are some really good ones, requiring reservations, but prices are relatively high.

Some hotels have excellent value "Eat-all-you-want" type restaurants, Holiday Inns and Hilton Inns particularly. Sunday 'brunch' is a popular American custom, with enormous spreads at a fixed price, available between 11 am and 3 pm. Most hotels feature two types of restaurant, an inexpensive coffee shop and a 'gourmet' restaurant, the latter not always worth the cost. In the larger cities, most of the cognoscenti go out to breakfast at nearby cafes, which will be much cheaper, quicker, and often better. This is very much the case in New York City where there are 13,000 cafes, stalls, and restaurants offering cooked breakfasts from $1.99 to $3.95.

The great American drug store has become an institution, although the best days are over. Selling a wide range of products and gadgets, some of the latter extremely popular with visitors from abroad, they invariably provide quick lunch (or 'soda') counters. They are not so popular these days in the face of cheaper competition from fast food chains, but they still make imaginative ice cream sundaes. The most famous drug store in America, possibly in the world, is Wall Drug, a huge emporium in the city of Wall, South Dakota (population 900), close to the Badlands. Advertisements for this store appear even on London buses ('you are only 5520 miles from Wall Drug Store') and on the underground trains in Sydney, Australia! It claims to sell the very last 5 cent coffee in USA but it makes its money from everything else, including fine ranges of Western clothes, and even four-wheel drive cars.

Wherever there is waitress service in a cafe or restaurant, the recognised tip is 15 percent of the check. At a gourmet spot with a waiter and a commie-waiter involving themselves at a reserved table, 20 percent is conventional. It is even desirable to tip at drug store counters and in diners, leaving a coin up to 10 percent of the check. Only in fast food or self service places is there no tipping.

Drink
Drinking laws throughout the United States are complicated in the extreme. Why any Americans visiting Europe should be critical of Britain or Scandinavia in this respect is puzzling, unless they only know their own State which may be very liberal. Briefly, there are still some 'dry' areas of the

country, where the repeal of Prohibition in 1933 was not applied by local vote. Totally dry (meaning no beer in excess of 3.2 percent alcohol) are Idaho, Utah, Oklahoma and large parts of Tennessee (the western end particularly), Arkansas, Kansas and Colorado. There can be private clubs in these areas where drinking may take place but they do require controlled membership; this can be liberally applied in some clubs.

Texas is a beer and wine only State. Many do not allow drinking on Sundays. Exactly 49 States impose a minimum age limit, varying from 18 to 21, and barmen will enforce it. Only Nevada is completely without restrictions, "anytime, anywhere, to anyone" their policy. New York is very liberal (8 am to 4 am subject to a minimum age of 18) while across the river, New Jersey is 9 am to 2 am. Carrying an open bottle of liquor in a car is a serious offence in some states, and importation from one to another, in quantity, is banned (although not strictly enforced, if found during a routine search, a gaol sentence could result).

Oddly enough – or perhaps not so – the only State where very few drunks are encountered is Nevada. The State of Washington will take steps to arrest anyone believed to be drunk on a Sunday. I recall attending a Convention in Seattle where, on the Sunday, the Swiss stand had a St Bernard dog carrying a small barrel round its neck. The police, routinely checking the hall, arrested the beast and took it Downtown for offering brandy on a Sunday. But it turned out the barrel contained only water and the police, somewhat shamefaced, drove it back to the hall!

Shopping

Shopping throughout America is undoubtedly the best in the world for choice and value for money. The Department Store was born in that country and exported (Selfridge was an American who set the pattern in Edwardian England). New York's famous Macy's and Bloomingdales represent the low level and high level in that city. Marshall Field in Chicago is a time-honoured big store. Every major city has a top grade one, and another with a bargain basement.

In every city and town, Friday evening is bargain time, the smaller towns seeing their stores put out bargain items on the sidewalk with up to 75 percent off. This is actually between 5.30 pm and 7 pm. Shops and stores stay open late by European standards, but the big ones tend to be closed on Saturday afternoons and Sundays. Nevertheless, widespread shopping is available outside Downtown areas on Sundays. The big supermarkets maintain a 24 hours service everday with shift work.

One other point about buying things is worth noting and that is the 'flea market' and 'garage sale'. It needs a car to find these and get the best from them as they will only be advertised on small noticeboards in the vicinity. At weekends in the suburbs of a major city from May to October, there may be as many as twenty garage sales (or yard sales) when residents put out their unwanteds at throw-away prices.

Bookshops are in abundance throughout America, averaging one for every 2000 people. Americans buy books rather than borrow them. Greater Boston has more bookshops than in the whole of London and the Home Counties, both used (second hand) and new, while the ubiquitous 'Book Exchange' stores are found in almost every suburb.

15.   Hotels, Motels, Lodges and Other Accommodation

Hotels/Motels

Nowhere on Earth has such a widespread choice of accommodation as the United States, from de luxe hotels to family lodges, at all kinds of prices. If a place is large enough to be marked on a map it will have at least two places to stay, even if it is only a small motel and a campground.

America is where the chain system of major hotels was first started. It is also the inventor of the motel. Recently, though, it has copied the European idea of bed and breakfast pensions and guest houses.

Immediately after the last war, the United States was lacking in decent family accommodation outside the main resort areas, and it is to the credit of Kemmons Wilson in 1950 who decided – after a disappointing tour when he felt he could not locate suitable places for his family to stay in comfort – to build the Holiday Inns. There are now nearly 1400 of them, although he is no longer directly connected with the business.

Every Holiday Inn on being franchised (very few are owned by the Company) must offer abundant free parking, 'king-sized' rooms capable of sleeping a family of two adults and two children, and 24 hour availability of hot food or beverages. In recent years another requirement is a swimming pool on the premises. Instant onward booking by way of Holidex in Memphis, free to the guest, must also be provided. Prices range very widely, from 37 Dollars a room in some Holiday Inns in the South and in Texas, to 120 Dollars or more in cities such as New York and Washington.

There are never 'No Vacancy' signs displayed outside. As Kemmons Wilson laid down in his policy: "Let them come in and find out. If we are full up we will call around and find some place with vacancies".

Hotel chains exist at all levels, from five star de luxe to simple one star establishments. The British company Trust House-Forte has the greatest number from top to bottom, with several 'Exclusive' hotels down through Excelsiors and Viscounts to the vast number of Travelodges. Level with TH-F's Exclusives are the Ritz–Carlton Group's fine establishments, the Hyatt Regency chain, and a few Westin's, plus the British-owned Hilton Vistas.

There are hundreds of Hiltons which belong to Mr Barron Hilton, son of the Founder (Conrad Hilton), and these operate at a much less lavish level. Some of the smaller Hilton Inns are on a cost-parity with smaller Holiday Inns.

Top ranking hotel chains below the de luxe level are the Marriotts (but a new upmarket number of these, described as Marriott Marquis hotels, are virtually up to the best in the country), the Sheratons, and the Ramada Renaissance establishments. The Omni chain is big and growing, while a few Best Westerns are up with the leaders.

Every part of the United States has its Quality Inns and Days Inns scattered around cities. There are almost as many Howard Johnsons, with distinctive red roofs, while more than 800 Trust House-Forte Travelodges controlled from a central reservation system in Kansas City directly linked to Ealing in West London are found from coast to coast. These hotels are mainly in the moderate price category.

The days of centrally located commercial hotels, based upon rail travel and guests walking across from the station, are almost gone. Except for the biggest cities, most hotels are somewhat away from central districts, based upon car travel. But there are numbers of low priced hotels close to Greyhound and Trailways bus terminals, to which passengers can walk with their baggage. These tend to be individually owned and would be rated one-star. A feature of low cost city hotels is the absence of service and restaurants, and the abundant green paint on walls.

It is extremely rare for a room to include breakfast; indeed this only happens in a resort area. Fully inclusive with meals, curiously called 'American Plan', is limited to major resort hotels. Nearly 99 percent are what is also curiously called 'European Plan', meaning room only. As for single rooms, they are becoming hard to find; most quotes are for a double room and it does mean that two can stay as cheaply as one. An exception to this is the business-oriented 'Motel 6' chain, which quotes really modest rates for single people in single rooms with no frills (an extra charge is made for TV set keys). The Motel 6's are invariably full and clearly indicate a demand for this kind of accommodation.

Individual travellers in the States will do well to choose motels, especially when using a car. There are tens of thousands of these places, usually set back a bit from highways and found in clusters at important cross-roads. When travelling with a colleague I have used motels literally hundreds of times, and always apply the same principles. No advance bookings are needed nor called for; one goes by the vacancy sign, lit at night. It is quite normal to drive up to the office and ask to see a room. The rates, if not quoted on the sign, should then be obtained. No offence is taken and no harm is done by driving away if not satisfied and your budget is not met.

Often it turns out that motels are owned as tax loss businesses by doctors and lawyers who rely on a resident clerk/manager and employ cleaning companies who turn up every morning. There is no way of telling except that the rates will be remarkably low (even now, 20 to 25 Dollars for a room with two beds, and sometimes free coffee on tap in the office area). All motels, like all hotels in the United States, provide private bathrooms, usually a shower rather than a tub.

From a car, to save driving in if on a budget, it can be seen if the motel is upmarket and fairly expensive. The 'Triple A' sign indicates this (American Automobile Association). Some show that they below to chains, Best Western being prevalent. In the South West, where rates are low in any case, the Friendship Inn establishments closely resemble motels. TraveLodges are usually two-storey buildings; they can range widely in price.

A quick check should be made before commitment that there are cafes or restaurants within easy walking distance or a short drive away. Motels rarely provide catering. Room money is always paid in advance when the key is handed over, and one drives to the room, parking outside. In the morning it is only necessary to leave the key in the lock and make a clean getaway, unless there are phone calls to pay for. If deciding to stay a second night, the money is paid before ten o'clock in the morning.

Other Accommodation

At a lower, and cheaper, level than motels are family lodges, invariably independently owned and usually built of wood. These will offer two rooms (plus private bath) and sometimes quote weekly rates. They will be found more often in resort areas, and are largely aimed at 'blue-collar' traffic with a family car-load. There is usually a facility for cooking in the rooms.

Another kind of lodge, also built of wood, is the often luxurious National Park or State Park establishment. Such places may provide the only available accommodation in the area and will cost more than motels. Really grand ones, such as those at Grand Canyon and Yellowstone Park, will be expensive, but will offer many facilities including coffee shops and restaurants (there may be nowhere else to eat for miles).

All over the States, especially in tourist areas, there are well constructed camp grounds for campers (caravans) and people pitching tents. Water and mains electricity can be plugged in and snack facilities are usually on site. There is a daily charge, modest enough, paid in advance at the office. Nowhere to my knowledge is there legal overnight camping on highways or on parking zones. Highway patrols will check and prevent this during the night.

As millions of Americans began to travel to Europe and became users of the bed and breakfast places they encountered all-over Britain, France, and some other continental countries, they brought home a demand for similar accommodation. In recent years this business has developed in the United States, particularly in New England and California.

Many old houses have been converted to offer bed and breakfast in charming surroundings, the rooms too often a bit 'chintzy' and usually with a ban on smoking. The breakfasts offered are massive American ones except in a few instances where no cooking is done but plenty of fruit and cereals are on the menu. There are farm houses, too, going in for this business and I was impressed by one in deep New England countryside 20 miles North of Montpelier, Vermont's small capital, where the views extended to the high hills of Canada on the Quebec border. Here the owners provided a country supper as well as breakfast. It is called the "Fitch House".

A number of bed and breakfast organisations have been formed to promote the scheme, and in California alone listing about 450, when only ten years ago there were none. Some have become allied with the British-based World Wide Bed and Breakfast Association. Prices are always based on two people sharing, and in New England start at about 28 Dollars, in California from 22 Dollars. Some very elaborate and carefully restored country houses, which put drinks in the rooms and supply many extra comforts, can cost 100 Dollars a night. They are invariably called inns and accept casual traffic.

Finding a place to stay at short notice when on tour with a car should not provide any problems except at a few peak periods. Always avoid chancing it throughout New England during the

Fall Foliage period (mid-September to mid-October) when large numbers of senior citizens are touring by bus and car. Peak weekends such as the Memorial day weekend (last weekend in May), July 4, and Labor Day (first weekend in September) are difficult, but Thanksgiving is easy since people tend to go home to families. This is the fourth Thursday, plus the weekend of November, when hotels will even offer cut rates. Big conventions fill all leading hotels for miles around at any time of year, but lower grade accommodation is not usually affected.

Many hotels in Florida have gone in for the long-stay package holiday business, for one or two weeks especially aimed at foreign visitors. These are arranged by tour operators, always on a room-only basis. In Miami I have actually seen hotels with signs up "a week for Fifty English Pounds" . . .

16.   Glossary of US Terminology

It is sometimes said of America and Britain that they are two nations divided by a single language. Many common words and several common expressions have totally different meanings, and it is well to be aware of them to avoid giving offence or to prevent serious misunderstandings.

An important difference is in telling the time, which has on occasions led to a wrong wake-up call in hotels with consequent missing of a flight or lateness for an appointment. Always stick to the 12-hour clock and quote time in the International manner, such as 7.45 or 11.15 or 3.30 pm. Americans say, when speaking colloquially, "a quarter of eight" for 7.45, and never "a quarter to eight" which some telephone operators – among others– interpret as 8.15. Similarly, the American interpretation of 8.20 will be "twenty after eight" and not "twenty past eight" although the latter is not usually misunderstood.

Using the telephone is straightforward and still very efficient compared with most of the world although it is less so than several years ago. The word 'trunk' is never used, 'long distance' being the correct expression, but 'toll call' is just the same as in Britain. Americans do not recognise the term 'ring me', always using the world 'call'. If physically calling, they say "I'll stop by."

Some American expressions are more accurate and logical than those Britons have used for generations.

Telling a child to 'stay on the pavement' may be life-preserving in Britain but could (and indeed has) lead to disaster in a busy US city. The term 'side-walk' is clear and positive; 'pavement' is obviously the road, once dirt, and subsequently paved over. Dust-bin may be a reasonable word but these big cans are more often filled with garbage, and Americans use the expression 'garbage can' and dustmen become 'garbage collectors', which is surely more suitable.

There are some cases where American expressions from the 1920's and 1930's have been found unsatisfactory, and have changed to more acceptable usage. Once, aircraft were 'ships' in USA, but now they are planes or jets. Two generations ago, all trousers were 'pants' but now, especially in the Eastern States, they are 'slacks' or trousers', but underpants for men are still undershorts. 'Candy' used to be used for all kinds of sweets and chocolates; now it applies only to the former. Wider travel by Americans has led to more universally understood adaptations, while TV importations from Britain have made accents better recognised.

The word "fortnight" has no meaning anywhere in America. Do not use it on an immigration form; put 'two weeks' instead. When filling OUT (never IN) such a form, put 'vacation' instead of holiday, which often refers to day trips. For unknown reasons the American word 'accommodations' is always used in the plural. It does not mean a list of places where you will be staying, but can be an apartment, a cruise ship cabin, a railroad sleeping berth, or hotel room. The expression 'Christian name' is not used – it is 'First name'.

Spelling and pronunciation are different at times but not unrecognisably so. Where English–English uses two 'L's, Americans mainly use one, and they frequently omit unnecessary letters such as a 'u' in harbour or labour. The common word 'got' mostly becomes 'gotten'. Irregularities may be abandoned, for example the 'sch' always 'ske' as in 'skedule' (but then the English say 'skeme').

Here are some American words and their English equivalents:-

Motoring/Driving

Rental car	hired car
Gasolene	petrol
Trunk	boot
Hood	bonnet
Windshield	windscreen
Fender	bumper
Sedan	saloon car
Limo	Big saloon with divider
Traffic Circle	roundabout
Divided highway	dual carriageway
Intersection	crossroads
Dead end street	Cul de Sac
Crosswalk (X-ing)	pedestrian crossing
Overpass	fly-over
Shift stick	car gear lever (non-auto)
Make/hang a right/left	turn right/left

Air Travel

Gate	Departure desk
Deplane	leave aircraft
Bumped	denied boarding (overbooked)
Non-Sched. flight	charter flight
Airplane	aeroplane
Field	small aerodrome

Rail Travel

Depot (often train-station)	railway station
Conductor	In charge of train (guard +)
Track 2, 3, 4 etc.	platform 2, 3, 4, etc.
Car	railway coach
Engineer	driver

Round trip ticket ....return ticket
One way ticket ....single ticket
Coach ticket ....standard seat ticket
Sleeper or parlor ....first class
Washroom ....toilet
Highball ....getting the green light
Commuter, an American word now fully
integrated into English–English, at first meaning
suburban train, honouring a ten-ride commuter ticket.

General Terms

Elevator ....lift
Maitre D'....................................head waiter
Longshoreman ....docker
Cornerstone ....Foundation stone
Drug Store...................................Chemist
Flashlight ....Torch
Diapers ....Nappies
Wash cloth ....Flannel
Purse..Handbag
Pocket Book.................................Wallet
Robe ....Dressing Gown
Drapes ....Curtains
Panty-hose ....Tights
Sneakers....................................Plimsolls
Vest ....Waistcoat
Garters ....Suspenders
Suspenders ....Braces
Faucet ....Tap
Socket ....Plug point
Regular......................................Standard or normal
Check.......................................Bank cheque or bill
Public School ....State school
Private School ....Public School
Yard ....Garden
Service Station ....Public garage
Jelly ....Jam
Jello ....Jelly
Dessert ....Sweet or pudding
Beverage....................................Tea or coffee with meal
Generator ....Includes car or bike dynamo
Pier...Berth or Dock
Shrimps (or Jumbo shrimps).................All shrimps and prawns
Excuse me ....Sorry
Expensive...................................Dear (not understood in this sense)
Cab ....Taxi (near extinct term in USA)
Eyeglasses ....Spectacles
Comforter (on a bed)........................Eiderdown

It is important to remember that in hotels, the first floor is, in English, the ground floor, and thus the second floor is the first floor in English. This confirms that most, but not all, American expressions are more logical, as with the sidewalk situation. 'Mezzanine' and 'Penthouse' are international.

On the telephone in contact with the operator, one asks for information (which is free), not Directory Enquiries. A reverse charges call is a collect call. A pay phone is one in a small open booth; a pay phone booth is what English people call a phone box.

In law, the term 'Barrister' is not understood, lawyers being both solicitors and spokespeople in Court. A Judge is addressed as 'Your Honor'. A city police station is known as a Precinct, usually numbered.

America uses only the fahrenheit scale for temperatures. Measurements, from inches to miles, are as in England. The US gallon, however, is only four/fifths of the Imperial gallon. The weight expression 'stone' is not used, only pounds.

Finally, when shopping, the expression 'cheap' will not be found. It does not mean 'Low cost', 'inexpensive', or 'bargain' but something rather nasty, even dishonourable.

17. Climate

There are twelve Major Natural Climatic Regions in the World, plus their various sub-divisions. The contiguous 48 States, excluding Alaska and Hawaii, are big enough to have eight of them, and with the addition of Canada and the Latin America countries down to Panama, the North American Continent has eleven. The USA including Alaska, with its cool temperate and arctic climates musters ten.

From the Canadian border in Maine down along the East Coast to Cape Hatteras on North Carolina's Outer Banks, we find the ST. LAWRENCE-MANCHURIAN CLIMATE.

From Cape Hatteras (where winds and currents mix) down to Daytona Beach in Florida, and also on the North shore of the Gulf of Mexico inclusive of West Florida, Mobile, New Orleans, and Houston, it is the WARM TEMPERATE CLIMATE.

South Florida down to the Keys, and including the Gulf Coast from Clearwater southwards, it is the TROPICAL CLIMATE (a sub-division allowing for occasional 'Northers' in winter). This climate is also found along the Texas Tropical Coast from Corpus Christi to Brownsville, and of course across into Mexico. All of the Hawaiian Islands belong to the tropical type, under trade wind influences.

The MEDITERRANEAN CLIMATE is well defined on the Pacific Coast from Cape Mendocino, northern California, down to San Diego.

The COOL TEMPERATE CLIMATE starts at Cape Mendocino (like Cape Hatteras on the Atlantic, another headland where winds and currents mix) and runs up the West Coast including the Pacific North West cities to Vancouver, BC.

A vast area of the South West between the Rockies and the Sierras experiences the HOT DESERT CLIMATE.

At higher altitudes and tending to be to the North of the hot deserts we find the TEMPERATE DESERT CLIMATE. This includes North Arizona, Utah and Colorado.

The largest area of all, covering all the great grasslands and Prairie, 2,500 miles North to South and at least 600 miles across, belongs to the CONTINENTAL GRASSLANDS CLIMATE. Dangerous tornadoes are experienced in the March-June period in southern areas.

Very high mountain ranges have, of course, their own sub-divisions according to altitude and latitude.

Taking a typical example from each of the eight, the monthly average maximum and minimum temperatures in degrees Fahrenheit, the monthly rainfall (which may be snow), and the relative humidity are shown in the following table. There are also notes on the particular characteristics of each climate.

Alaska has the COLD TEMPERATE CLIMATE (Anchorage and Fairbanks) with long cold winters, a short warm summer, and brief transition seasons. It also has the *ARCTIC CLIMATE* in the far North, where the permafrost keeps it cool to cold all year, with some warm days in high summer and very little rain or snow. What snow does fall lays and stays all Winter (September to May).

Climatic Types

Example   Jan Feb Mar Apr May June July Aug Sept Oct Nov Dec

St. Lawrence–Manchurian

New York City

37/24 38/24 45/30 57/42 68/53 78/60 83/67 80/66 74/60 64/49 51/37 41/29
3.7" 3.8" 3.6" 3.2" 3.2" 3.3" 4.2" 4.3" 3.4" 3.5" 3.0" 3.6"

Humidity high every month, peaking in July and August with 73% and 76%

The St Lawrence/Manchurian type is noted for cold winters, hot and humid summers, very pleasant lengthy autumns, and an evenly distributed fairly heavy rainfall.

Warm Temperate (Gulf subdivision)

New Orleans

63/48 65/50 71/55 77/61 83/68 88/74 90/76 89/76 86/73 78/64 70/54 63/48
4.6" 4.3" 5.0" 5.3" 5.0" 5.6" 6.6" 6.0" 5.1" 3.7" 3.5" 4.6"

Humidity high every month at an even 78%

The Warm Temperate type has heavy summer rains, the summers very hot and humid, the autumn usually pleasant. Frost and snow are rare; there is some hurricane risk from August to October.

Tropical

Miami

76/59 77/59 80/63 83/67 85/71 88/74 89/76 90/76 88/75 85/71 80/65 77/60
2.2" 2.0" 2.1" 3.6" 6.1" 9.0" 6.9" 6.7" 8.7" 8.2" 2.7" 1.6"

Humidity moderate in winter, high in summer, very high in autumn

The Tropical type is characterised in USA by summer and autumn rains, dry winters. It is always warm or hot. There is a risk of hurricanes between August and November.

Mediterranean

Los Angeles

67/47 68/49 69/50 71/53 73/56 77/60 83/64 84/64 83/63 78/59 73/52 68/48
3.0" 2.8" 2.2" 1.3" 0.1" Nil Nil Nil 0.2" 0.3" 2.0" 2.2"

Humidity moderate in winter, low in summer, sometimes only 20%

The Mediterranean type has long hot dry summers, short mild wet winters, a negligible spring, but a pleasant two months of autumnal transition.

Cool Temperate

Seattle

44/33 47/35 51/36 58/40 66/45 70/50 76/54 75/54 69/51 60/44 50/38 46/35
5.7" 4.2" 3.8" 2.4" 1.7" 1.6" 1.0" 1.1" 2.1" 4.0" 5.4" 6.3"

Humidity fairly high in winter, moderate in summer

The Cool Temperate type (found in NW Europe among other places) is not extreme, has relatively heavy winter rains and light summer rains, a very pleasant spring. There can be cold spells in winter with snow, and heat waves in summer.

Hot Desert

Phoenix

65/38 69/41 75/45 84/52 93/60 102/68 105/78 102/76 98/69 88/57 75/45 66/39
0.7" 0.6" 0.5" 0.3" 0.1" 0.1" 0.8" 0.9" 0.8" 0.5" 0.5" 0.8"

Humidity very low all year, sometimes only 20%

The Hot Desert type has a wide daily range of temperature with chilly winter nights. Rainfall is mostly from heavy thunderstorms (flash flood dangers) and may not occur at all in two years, with a relatively wet third year producing the averages.

Example	Jan	Feb	Mar	Apr	May	June	July	Aug	Sept	Oct	Nov	Dec

Temperate Desert

Grand Canyon	41/16	43/18	53/25	55/27	73/39	75/41	84/51	86/52	68/43	65/40	51/24	48/22
	0.2"	0.1"	0.3"	0.3"	0.5"	0.6"	0.3"	0.4"	0.3"	0.5"	0.6"	0.7"

Humidity low all year round, often below 25%

The Temperate Desert is found at altitude, and usually has bitterly cold nights in winter (the frosts shaping desert rocks). Rain (it may be snow) is minimal.

Continental Grasslands

Kansas City	36/19	42/24	51/32	65/45	74/56	83/65	88/70	87/68	79/59	69/48	53/35	40/24
	1.3"	1.3"	2.6"	3.5"	4.3"	5.6"	4.4"	3.8"	4.2"	3.2"	1.5"	1.5

The humidity is high (over 65%) in early summer, moderate rest of year

Dallas	56/34	60/38	67/43	76/54	83/62	90/69	96/74	96/74	89/67	79/56	68/44	59/37
	1.8"	2.4"	2.5"	4.3"	4.5"	3.1"	1.8"	2.3"	3.2"	2.7"	2.0"	1.8"

Humidity moderate, sometimes high in early summer. Range 40% to 75%

The Continental Grasslands are characterised by early summer rains (good for the wheat), and hot to very hot summers. In the North of the region, very cold winters are experienced, with temperatures at times down to minus 40 degrees. Bismarck, North Dakota's capital, has had a summer maximum of 105 degrees and a minimum of minus 46 IN THE SAME YEAR. The Southern Grasslands are prone to spring tornadoes.

Finally, the Federal Capital of Washington, in a southerly section of the St Lawrence/Manchurian climate, is shown in detail. This city is acknowledged to have, for about six months of the year, one of the worst climates in the United States and indeed some foreign embassy staffs including the British were paid 'weather compensation' accordingly.

Washington DC	41/23	43/24	53/31	65/41	75/51	83/59	86/64	85/64	79/55	68/44	56/34	43/25

Rainfall totalling 40 inches annually, is fairly even with a summer peak. Humidity is cruelly high in summer, up to 90%. Mid September to mid November, and late April to late May are the best times to visit.

18. Dates in American History

1492	Christopher Columbus lands in Bahamas.
1497	John Cabot explored North East Coast of America.
1513	Ponce de Leon explored coast of Florida.
1565	Pedro Menendez founded St Augustine, Florida.
1587	First British Colony, Roanoke Is., (then Virginia).
1607	Capt. John Smith founded Jamestown, Virginia.
1609	Dutch employee, Henry Hudson, sailed into New York.
1620	Pilgrim Fathers arrived at Plimoth, Massachusetts.
1630	Massachusetts Bay Co. founded Boston.
1634	Calvert's Catholics founded St Mary's, South Maryland.
1636	Harvard College founded near Boston, Mass.
1664	British seized New York from Dutch.
1683	William Penn bought Pennsylvania from Delaware Indians.
1740	Capt. Vitus Bering (Dane in Russian service) sailed to Alaska.
1754–1761	Seven Years War with French; British took Quebec; moved French from Arcadia to Louisiana; French lost all mid-America.
1773	Boston Tea Party; American revolt against tea tax.
1775	Beginning of American War of Independence.
1776	American Declaration of Independence.
1781	Cornwallis surrenders and ends War; Britain recognise Independence of the United States.
1789	General George Washington resigned commission in State House, Maryland; later chosen as President.
1796	Washington's Farewell Address as President.
1804	Lewis & Clarke expedition sent to explore the vast territories of the Louisiana Purchase (from French) the year before.
1812–14	War with Britain; in 1813 British burned Capitol and White House in Washington. War ended with Treaty of Ghent, declared a draw.
1819	US bought Florida from Spain.
1828/1829	Baltimore & Ohio Railroad begun; first passengers.
1836	Siege of Alamo, Texas, followed by defeat of Mexicans at San Jacinto. Texas Independence.
1845	Texas joins the United States.
1846	Oregon Territory armed dispute with Britain over '54.50' Expansionist claim. Latitude 49 degrees fixed in Britain's favour.
1849	Gold Rush to California; some 80,000 '49ers' dig.
1860–61	The Pony Express, mail service from Mississippi to California; worked for 18 months, no casualties.
1861	Start of the War Between the States.
1863	Confederate Army defeated at Gettysburg; Lincoln's Address.

1865	End of War with surrender of Lee at Appomatox, Va.
1867	Purchase of Alaska from Russia.
1871	Great Fire of Chicago; every building bar one destroyed.
1873	First US post card issued.
1876	General Custer wiped out by Sioux at Little Big Horn.
1879	First Woolworth store opened (in Utica, New York).
1883	Brooklyn Bridge opened from Manhattan to Brooklyn.
1889	The Johnstown Flood, Penn; 2200 drowned.
1890	Battle of Wounded Knee, S. Dakota, the last of the major Indian Wars, with US troops.
1898	Spanish–American War. Spain lost Cuba, Puerto Rico, the Phillipines and Guam. Hawaii annexed by USA.
1903	US formally took over Panama Canal project from French; created Republic of Panama from Columbia. First powered flight by Wright Brothers.
1906	San Francisco Earthquake and fire.
1911	First trans-Continental airplane flight (82¼ hours).
1914	Panama Canal opened.
1916	General Pershing invades Mexico to put down Villa. US bought three Virgin Islands from Denmark.
1917	US enters Great War against Germany.
1919	Over 1 million US troops back from France. Prohibition begins.
1921	Immigration quotas established.
1927	First solo flight, US to Europe by Capt. Lindbergh. The "Jazz Singer" with Al Jolson, first talking picture.
1929	The October Wall Street Crash. Depression started.
1931	Empire State Building opened, despite Depression.
1933	President Roosevelt orders closure of all US Banks; Stayed shut 100 days. Federal Prohibition ended.
1941	Japanese attacked Pearl Harbor. US at war with Japan and Germany (December).
1944	The Anglo-American Normandy Invasion (June 6).
1945	End of War with Germany (May); first Atomic Bomb exploded at Alamagordo, New Mexico, (July); Japan surrenders after two more Atomic Bombs dropped.
1946	Bretton Woods financial agreement; Phillipines independent.
1950–51	Korean War
1958	First US satellite launched into space. First jet flight in USA on commercial service; first to UK in October.
1959	Alaska and Hawaii admitted as States of the Union.
1962	John Glenn first US man in Space to orbit Earth.
1963	Assassination of J. F. Kennedy, President, in Dallas.
1969	First landing on the Moon.
1963–1973	The Vietnam War. Ended with defeat and withdrawal of US troops from Saigon March 29.
1971	AMTRAK (National Railroad Passenger Corporation) begins.
1974	President Nixon resigns after Watergate scandal.
1976	Bicentennial Year. Mammoth nationwide celebrations.

TOP TRAVEL TITLES FROM SETTLE PRESS

The following books all feature in the highly popular WHERE TO GO IN series.

WHERE TO GO IN GREECE
by Trevor Webster
An up-to-date, easy-to-read, illustrated guide to
the islands and mainland centres.

£12.50 hard 0907070841 ☐
£7.99 paper 0907070876 ☐
New Edition
April 1991

"an exceptional title for both those seeking culture
and the sun". *The Bookseller*

WHERE TO GO IN ROMANIA
by Harold Dennis-Jones
An up-to-date post-revolution guide book from an
author whose recent journeys in Romania are the
culmination of 24 years of visits.

£14.00 hard 090707071X ☐
£8.99 paper 0907070728 ☐
Publication January 1991

WHERE TO GO IN SCOTLAND
by Bryn Frank
The myths, the magic and the taste (food and drink)
are all included in this clear guide to the Scottish
regions.

£12.50 hard 0907070884 ☐
£7.99 paper 0907070892 ☐
Publication June 1991

**CRETE AND THE CYCLADES
ISLANDS**
by Trevor Webster
The atmosphere of their stupendous mountains,
beaches, harbours and history is relayed by Trevor
Webster.

£9.99 hard 0907070388 ☐
£6.99 paper 0907070396 ☐
1987

WHERE TO GO IN SPAIN
A guide to the Iberian peninsula
by H. Dennis-Jones
Includes rating guides for all the Spanish coastal
regions and colourful descriptions of the interior.

£9.99 hard 0907070426 ☐
£5.99 paper 0907070434 ☐
1987

WHERE TO GO IN THE CANARY ISLANDS
by Reg Butler
Jetset nightlife, or peace-and-quiet; dramatic scenery
or city sightseeing and shopping – The Canary
Islands can help you choose which island can best fill
your requirements.

£14.00 hard 0907070671 ☐
£8.99 paper 090707068X ☐
1990

WHERE TO GO IN TUNISIA
by Reg Butler
While most visitors choose Tunisia for its year-round
Mediterranean sunshine, the book also describes the
fascination of Roman remains, Islamic cities, country
markets, oases and Berber strongholds.

£14.00 hard 0907070485 ☐
£8.99 paper 0907070493 ☐
1990

GREEK ISLAND DELIGHTS
by Trevor Webster
Trevor Webster explores 12 of the most popular and
magical isles in Greece, Crete, Corfu, Rhodes, Kos,
Samos, Skiathos, Mykonos, Santorini, Paros,
Thassos, Kephalonia and Zakynthos.

£14.00 hard 0907070604 ☐
£8.99 paper 0907070612 ☐

SETTLE PRESS (Reader Service Dept.), 10 Boyne Terrace Mews, London W11 3LR

Please send me the book(s) I have ticked. I am enclosing £
(prices cover postage and handling in UK).

Mr/Mrs/Miss . . . .

Address . . . .

. . . .

. . . .